Loving God: Living with Cancer

Loving GOD:
Living with Cancer

Judy Hindy, RN, MSN

XULON PRESS

Xulon Press
2301 Lucien Way #415
Maitland, FL 32751
407.339.4217
www.xulonpress.com

© 2022 by Judy Hindy, RN, MSN

All rights reserved solely by the author. The author guarantees all contents are original and do not infringe upon the legal rights of any other person or work. No part of this book may be reproduced in any form without the permission of the author.

Due to the changing nature of the Internet, if there are any web addresses, links, or URLs included in this manuscript, these may have been altered and may no longer be accessible. The views and opinions shared in this book belong solely to the author and do not necessarily reflect those of the publisher. The publisher therefore disclaims responsibility for the views or opinions expressed within the work.

Unless otherwise indicated, Scripture quotations taken from the Holy Bible, New International Version (NIV). Copyright © 1973, 1978, 1984, 2011 by Biblica, Inc.™. Used by permission. All rights reserved.

Paperback ISBN-13: 978-1-6628-4668-7
Ebook ISBN-13: 978-1-6628-4669-4

The Diagnosis of Cancer

Nothing changes a life when you hear the words, "you have cancer". This became a reality for me when I was diagnosed with stage IV colon cancer in August 2015. The first thing people think about who get diagnosed with a terminal disease is dying. Honestly, I was in complete shock when I was told that I had cancer after waking up from having a routine colonoscopy. This was the hardest day I had to face in my life.

First, I am the mother of three amazing boys, and I love them with all my heart. When I was diagnosed with cancer my oldest son, Joseph, was a senior in high school. He played basketball, baseball, and was on a travel baseball team, the Macomb Sting. He is a bright young man who was getting straight A's in school and looking at colleges where he could play baseball too. He loved baseball and was the starting pitcher for our high school team at Algonac High School. His dream was to become a chemical engineer and play baseball while pursuing his degree. He is also a good kid, never gets in any trouble, and loves the Lord. He served in our church to help with the audiovisual for Sunday services.

His faith in God is what directed his path to stand out among the kids who followed the crowd. He fills my life with joy. My second son, Thomas, is a strong willed, determined, and outgoing young man. He was a sophomore in high school who played basketball, baseball, and was on a travel baseball team, the Macomb Sting. He had no plans on continuing baseball at the college level, his dream was to become a doctor. He also obtained all A's in school and served in our church as an usher for Sunday's church services. He enjoyed high school and had a great group of friends. He loves the Lord and demonstrates this love by his character around his friends and in school. I love Thomas more than he realizes and always helped him to be the best he could be. My third son, Joshua, was in the sixth grade going to Algonquin Middle School. He did not find sports amusing and took an interest in music. He played in the church band the trumpet, bass, and helped with the audiovisuals. Joshua was my all around highly intelligent, happy go lucky kid. He always made me laugh and yet has a very tender heart. He can tell you a lot about each freighter that passes by our house, loves history, science, and is an extremely fast learner. The boys think he's my favorite but honestly, I love them all deeply from the bottom of my heart. My husband, David, is a strong leader of our home. He works many hours as a family physician. At times I struggled with just how many hours he worked while raising three boys, but he always made time for our family a priority. He was very

Table of Contents

The Diagnosis of Cancer 1
Moving Forward 11
Facing Chemotherapy 19
The Importance of Family Support 23
The Process Leading Up to Chemotherapy 25
Battle Time. 29
Colon Resection. 37
Sigmoid Resection 39
Recovery from Surgery 43
Changing the Chemotherapy Treatment 45
Graduation 2016 47
Hindy Strong Scholarship 51
God is Our Foundation 55
Understanding a Patient's Journey. 59
I am in a Dark Place. 65
Preparing for Another Surgery. 71
Time for Surgery 79
Recovery from Liver Resection Surgery 91
The Year's Ending Celebration 95
2017 A year of Change. 97

Grandma's Stroke 101

Radiation Therapy 105

Still More Tragedy 109

Can We Get a Break? 113

More Radiation Therapy 117

2018 Florida Trip 121

Graduation 2018 125

Ongoing Treatment 129

Feelings after Treatment 133

2019 Still more Chemotherapy 135

A Well Needed Break 137

PET Scan June 2019 141

COVID-19 Hits 143

COVID Diagnosis March 2021 149

Spring Break Vacation 157

Home Sweet Home 161

Time to Rest 167

Cancer Can't Take Away Time with Joe 171

Cancer Can't Take Away Joe with Thomas 177

Cancer Can't Stop Me from Smiling and
    Laughing with Joshua 181

Cancer Can't Stop Love with 26 Years
    of Marriage 185

Loving God: Living with Cancer 187

The Diagnosis of Cancer

active in our boy's baseball programs and taught them how to handle the ups and downs of winning and defeat. He taught them to face the challenges of baseball and life. Most importantly, he taught them about God and what it means to be a Godly man. He made sure we were in church every Sunday even when we were too tired to get out of bed. We even picked up grandpa and grandma along the way. Dave also served within our community as a doctor, coach, elder in our church, and mentor to so many kids. He was a great husband and always supported me within our home, with the kids, and my nursing career. He was never afraid to help me around the house, go grocery shopping, fix things that were broken or do anything that needed to be done. He was amazing with the boys and taught them how to be honorable young men by his example through his great character. We were incredibly blessed that grandpa and grandma lived near us. We were always together, and my boys were spoiled with grandma's great Lebanese cooking. Grandpa always had great stories about the war, growing up in the depression, and taught them about the Bible. He never had a college education, but I believed he was the smartest man I've ever met next to my husband. He also had a warm and loving heart that was always willing to help others. Grandma was a workhorse, she never complained, was never tired, and was always willing to help us out with anything. She was a tough person who migrated here from Lebanon and did not have an easy life. She came here with grandpa after they were married. I loved having them in our lives because it taught my kids about their culture, deepened their faith, and showered them with an abundance of love. I truly had a good life and so much love.

I loved being a wife, mother, and a nurse. Dave supported me when I decided to advance my degree to obtain my Master's in Nursing Education. It took me three years, but it was worth it when I started working for St. Clair Community college as a Clinical Instructor. I did that along with working in the ICU at River District Hospital. I loved nursing and I loved teaching. I wanted my students to respect the profession and most importantly to have empathy for those they serve. Nurses take care of people of different cultures, religions, beliefs, financial statuses, and health care needs. I've always taught them that each person is an individual and must be cared for according to their needs. I did not want them to just look at the graphics, labs, x-rays, or other test results but to look at them as individuals. I wanted them to look at their hair, skin, facial features, but most importantly listen to what they said. Many patients do not get better or become non-compliant because we miss the most crucial element of their healthcare and that is their mental, emotional, spiritual, and cognitive health. We treat them as if they are a textbook case and forget that they are a human being. They exist for a purpose, have value, and give meaning to others. We need to treat the whole person not just their disease. I was passionate about teaching, and it hurt me greatly the day I had to give it all up.

Faith in God has always been the most important thing in my life. My faith is the core of who I am, and it has guided all my decisions. In fact, the most important reason I married Dave was that he was a man of God and I wanted to grow in my faith with him. I am not a perfect person, don't get me wrong, I've made plenty of mistakes in my life, but my faith is what leads me to make changes to honor God. I love God and serve Him as a wife, mother, and in all I do. If I did not know the Lord, my cancer diagnosis would have been even more devastating. I know that when I die, as a Christian, I will spend eternity with God in Heaven and I'm not sure everyone can say that without doubt. It's not about just being a good person and all the things we do here on earth. We are saved through faith alone in Jesus Christ and it's through that faith and love that we honor God in how we love others. We honor God in how we live, what we do, and how we serve this world. I serve God by being the best wife, mother, and person I can be. We all sin but God sent His son Jesus Christ to die on the cross for our sins and we are forgiven. His Grace is sufficient for us, and we love because He first loved us. We live for purpose and passion because of what Jesus did on the cross. My purpose was my husband, family, and all the people I served along the way. God gave me the strength to handle my cancer diagnosis and everything I had to handle going forward.

Being diagnosed with cancer when my kids were so young was most devastating. I was very health-conscious person. I followed my beliefs as a nurse and exercised, kept my weight down, ate a well-balanced diet, and followed the recommendations of my doctors. Cancer was a major blow because I was young, healthy, and happy. Now, let me take you back to that day.

I was diagnosed with cancer just after we came home from a fantastic vacation in Myrtle Beach for a baseball tournament with our family. We had a beautiful condominium on the ocean with separate bathrooms, washer dryer, living room, and kitchen. We went all out making this a special time for our family We had so much fun as a family and with the team. Our vacation ended with wonderful memories, but life moves on, and we had to get back to our lives in Algonac. I was getting ready for another semester teaching at St. Clair Community College, working in the ICU, and the kids were going back to school. One of the recommendations for health screening is to have a colonoscopy at the age of 50. I had turned 50 in February, so I made sure to schedule this when we returned from our vacation. I honestly didn't think it was a big deal, just another test. The day before the procedure was schedule, I had to cleanse my colon with a clear liquid diet, take MiraLAX, and stool softeners. Dave drove me to the hospital very early in the morning. Thanks to grandpa and grandma, I did not have to worry about the kids. I felt at ease because I knew the doctor and nurses.

The Diagnosis of Cancer

That morning was a turning point in my life. After being prepped for the procedure, I was taken back to the procedure room. All I remember is the bright lights over my head, the equipment around the room, and watching the anesthesiologist giving me medication in my IV that put me to sleep. When I woke up, I still was very dazed. Dave was standing next to me when the doctor arrived to tell us about what she saw. She had tears in her eyes as she told us that I had a tumor in my colon so large that she could not get a pediatric scope past it so she couldn't complete the procedure. She believed it was colon cancer and I had to have a CT scan to see if the cancer progressed to other parts of my body. Dave and I were in complete shock. I listened to the doctor's words, but I could not process them or even cry. I was still disorientated from the anesthesia; however, I noticed the nurses were crying as they were getting me ready for a CT scan. After my scan, Dave broke the news that I had around 20 small tumors in my liver. The oncologist was working in his office next to the hospital came over to talk to Dave and I. Honestly, I do not even remember what he told us. All I wanted to know was if I would live to see my son Joseph graduate from high school. I just love Dr. Kahn, he was the kindest, most softspoken doctor I've known. With the most empathetic voice and concern for me, he looked me directly in the eyes and assured me I would see my son graduate. I didn't know if I truly believed him, but he gave me hope, and sometimes it's that hope that gives you the purpose to live and the willingness to fight.

I was emotionally at the lowest point of my life, and I needed to talk to Dr. Wayne, my family doctor, to help me process the next steps I would take in my cancer journey. When I called him, he took my call right away, and talked to me as if he had nothing else to do. I felt comfortable talking with him because he was the doctor who delivered my kids, worked with Dave for many years, and was a Godly man. I sobbed as I told him everything that happened. He calmed me down and helped me process the next steps I. He was instrumental in my cancer journey and now as I look back, I see the hand of God in that very awful day. God was present with the doctor and staff during my procedure. God shined His light when the oncologist was able to clear his schedule to talk to me the very same day. God's voice was heard when my family doctor calmed me down and assisted me with what to do next. God is always there, in good and bad times. He never leaves you and you can hear His voice when you listen. God shines the light of hope and walks with you through all your struggles. God has always been there for me my whole life and I know He will never leave me. He will guide me until I join Him in Heaven. I serve an awesome God, I may not always get everything I desire, but He gives me everything I need. His love and grace have carried me through this journey.

The Diagnosis of Cancer

After the initial panic, I realized I serve a great God, and this changed my perspective. I knew I could not do this alone. God gave me His love, strength, courage, and hope during this difficult time. He is the light in the darkness. The journey of cancer is different for everyone who goes through it, but when you have God, all things are possible. The biggest fear I had to face was that of dying. I faced that fear head on with knowing that if I should die, I will live forever with God in Heaven, so it brought me great peace. God has a plan for all of us, so I decided that it was time to let go and give this to God. Letting go of control was not easy. My whole life had been about control and being the mom who everyone could depend on. It was difficult to drop the reigns and give that control to God. Yet, I knew that this was way too big for me to handle alone, even with a supportive family. I realized that my cancer journey was going to be about loving God and living with cancer. I love God, trust Him with my life, and rely on Him to show me how I would go forward with living with stage IV colon cancer. I give God all the glory and I have learned to sit in the back seat and allow God to drive. He is my God whom I love, and I will learn to trust and rely on Him for everything in my life.

Moving Forward

After the diagnosis, I was faced with making many difficult decisions. The next difficult decision was figuring out how I would tell my children this devastating news. This was the most heart wrenching discussion I ever had with them. What led the discussion was our faith in Christ. We believe God has a plan for us and we must be obedient in what we need to do. We came home and gathered them around the living room and prayed. I can't tell you exactly how it all was said but we stressed the importance of our faith in God. I told them that I would need their support more than ever before and that we would face this as a family with the help of God. Our boys were understandably disheartened. Cancer effects the whole family, and it changes life for everyone involved. However, as difficult as this is, life must go on. We still had lives to live and must continue with work, school, church, and all our activities. It was not time to fall apart, stop life, and it was especially not time to give up. It was time to prepare for battle.

When you prepare for battle, you arm yourself. I put on the armor of God and looked to Him as my commander. I knew it wasn't going to be easy and there were no guarantees. No one is promised tomorrow. Each day is a blessing, and how we live our life here is what makes it all worth it. I live to honor God in all I do. I honor Him in my attitude, and I promised Him that if I could get through this, I would use this journey to bring people to Him. That is the biggest change I have seen in myself during this journey. I am living with a new purpose, and I am using my story as a testament to the awesome power of God. I am living as an example to lead people to the Lord.

We have a great family, not always perfect, but filled with a lot of love. As difficult as it was telling my kids that their mom had cancer, I knew they had a relationship with the Lord, and He would always be with them. Dave and I raised our boys in faith, they understand that we will not be on earth forever, and that our greatest place is with the Lord in Heaven. It comforts them knowing that when I die, I will be with the Lord, and one day they too will be with me because they have accepted Jesus into their hearts. Leaning on our faith was a huge comfort for my family. However, we resolved to face this journey as a family. As a family, we spent many years watching them play baseball. With each game we have learned many life lessons about courage, a positive attitude, and a determination to win. We know that life is not always easy, situations are not

Moving Forward

always ideal, and life can send you a curve ball. There are many hard-fought battles in both winning and losing. Competition is steep, coaches are demanding, umpires can make poor calls, and the team can be divided. The most important lesson we have learned is that we never quit. Above all, we love one another as a family. It's that love we have received from Christ that will keep us going strong, and it's that love we have for each other that will keep us together always.

After telling my kids about my cancer, the next step was telling the rest of our family and friends. I let Dave tell his parents and his siblings what happened. They were terribly upset, and all prayed for us. I told my family which consisted of three sisters and two brothers. After we told our extended family, the next call was to my manager at the hospital and the nursing director at the college. I had no choice but to quit both my jobs. I couldn't continue working because my doctor was planning for an aggressive chemotherapy treatment schedule. We didn't believe I would be in any condition to do my job duties. It was a difficult decision because I had worked for over 30 years in the hospital setting and it took me 13 years to obtain my BSN in nursing. I didn't have too much time to say goodbye to my coworkers because I was already scheduled for many doctors' appointments, laboratory tests, liver biopsy, and a mediport insertion procedure.

The mediport was put in my chest so I could receive the chemotherapy directly to my bloodstream without having to have an IV placed in smaller veins. The mediport is placed in the upper portion of the chest and allows access to the internal jugular vein which ends up going directly to the heart. I had a lot on my plate to do just before the kids were scheduled to return to school. Thankfully, Dave was able to take off work for every doctor's appointment and every procedure going forward. God was instrumental in him having an amazing staff that supported him and opened his schedule so we could make all our necessary appointments. I believed that following up with appointments is crucial in the outcome of this disease. It is not wise to put things off or not become informed. It's vital to learn as much as you can with what the doctors are telling you. It's important to write down questions, look up any medications you will be taking, and discussing everything with the doctor. Yes, Google may provide a huge range of information, but it should not be a substitute for the doctor. You need to discuss everything with the doctor including how you are doing emotionally. Your mental, emotional, and spiritual health is crucial to accepting your disease and begin moving forward. Some people become angry and question why this has happened to them. Others may go into complete denial and become non-compliant with the treatment program. However, I feel it's imperative to discuss those feelings with your doctor or someone professionally who can guide you through those feelings.

Moving Forward

My cancer diagnosis was a complete shock and blindsided both me and my family. There is never a good time to hear the diagnosis of cancer. I had so many questions and concerns that overwhelmed me. What I didn't understand is that there is no known colon cancer diagnosis in my family. My mother had died from breast cancer at the age of 62. The only other problem with obtaining a family history is that many of my relatives didn't have yearly physicals, exams, tests, or were educated about their health care needs. Many blood tests, exams, treatments in my parents' days were not available. Medical research was extremely limited, and doctors didn't have the resources they do today to treat people with major illnesses. Most people didn't even have health care, money, or means to meet their health care needs. Still others didn't even go to a doctor unless they were extremely ill while relying on home remedies for a cure. All these things made it difficult to assemble a family medical history. We are truly fortunate to have treatments and so many options today, so I feel extremely Blessed by God. My mother had a ninth-grade education, so she didn't even understand what breast cancer was about let alone have preventative care to screen for her health care needs. When she was diagnosed, she was incredibly angry and didn't follow up with the doctor as he made his recommendations. She didn't take care of her health and eventually the cancer took over and she died a few years after being diagnosed. This was most difficult for me as a young lady to watch my mom struggle with this. My siblings and I had to be her care givers until the end of her life. I believe this experience sparked my interest in nursing and preventative health care. I have seen so many people in the hospital who suffered greatly because they didn't follow up with their physician or do what they recommended. Moving forward is all about accepting your diagnosis and doing what is necessary to get better. This is no easy task, and it requires a lot of support from everyone around you.

I saw the hand of God through so many people who showed me love and support. The nurses I worked with at the college sent me many special get-well cards. My co-workers in the hospital sent me beautiful gifts that touched my heart. My students were so kind and one day a few of them stopped by to cheer me up. The people in my church were instrumental in praying for me, sending me cards, and holding me up when I was at my lowest point of my journey. My pastor prayed with me many times, listened to me cry, and was always there for me and my family. Deacon Dave and his wife Jan saved me so many times with scripture versus, prayers, and walking besides me as Christ would do. My family was always by my side and showed me unconditional love and support. Not everyone is so fortunate to have this blessing, so I felt extremely thankful moving forward. I didn't want to let all these people down when they surrounded me with so much love. I wanted to show my gratitude by showing them I could be strong and courageous. I would do what I had to do to survive and lean on God's understanding, not mine. I moved forward with the love of so many people, how could I fail or falter? I was a nurse so I knew how staying positive, taking care of myself along the way, and doing what was required would assist me in a better outcome. Moving forward, I relied on God to lead me the way. I knew He loved me, I was His child, I had a relationship with Him, and I loved Him with all my heart. I promised God that if I survived this that I would bring more people to Him and I would honor Him all the days of my life. Sin does exist in this world so bad things do happen. We can't focus on the why because we will never truly understand God's plan. All we can rely on is His love, guidance, and promise that one day we will be in Heaven with Him for eternity. In Heaven we don't have to worry about sin, sickness, or anything we struggle with here on earth. We will be eternally with God and that is our greatest hope moving forward.

Facing Chemotherapy

After being diagnosed with stage IV colon cancer, I didn't have much time to waste. I had to start chemotherapy right away. It was a whirlwind of ongoing steps leading up to this. I spent many days in tears, fearing what I was about to endure. When picturing someone going through chemotherapy one typically conjures up images of a bald, skinny, sickly looking individual. I tried to not go there with facing chemotherapy. I was willing to do whatever I had to do to beat this. I spent my days praying and depending on God to lead me through this. When you get diagnosed with cancer, people seem to want to help by giving you advice. I knew they meant well, but it became overwhelming with the information they were providing me. They would tell me to eat a certain diet, take certain supplements, about new studies using stem cells, and made many suggestions that it made me think my doctors didn't know what they were doing. I trusted my doctors and felt that all my treatments would be according to the plan we agreed on. This journey is very personal and complicated so as much as people mean well, it became a thorn in my side when someone tried to tell me they found a miraculous cure.

We had a lot on our plates with three boys who were involved in sports, school, and church activities. I didn't know how we were going to juggle all of this with my treatment plan. What I decided to do was take it one step at a time. I was on information overload trying to read things about my cancer. I was fortunate to have a team of doctors who were the absolute best and I trusted with my life. One of the first doctors we saw was Dr. Berri, who serves as the Chief of Surgical Oncology. He was soft spoken, kind, and gave me so much hope. He discussed the many options I had, and we decided that chemotherapy would be the best option at this point. The tumor was so large that it nearly obstructed my colon, there were other tumors in my lymph nodes, and more in my liver. He made me feel so much better after our discussion. The best thing he told me was not to pay attention to the research studies that told me that I had a high chance of dying. He told me that I'm not a statistic and those studies I was reading were not up to date. He believed I could get through this and set me up to have a mediport placement that same week. He was not going to waste any time with me because he knew I needed to start chemotherapy as soon as possible. The night before my procedure, I woke up in the middle of the night buckled over with abdominal pain. I broke out in a cold sweat and wanted Dave to take me to the emergency room. He called Dr. Berri, and he suggested I go to the emergency room too. I have had these symptoms before when I was under a lot of stress but not to this degree. I ended up taking some Tums and Gas-ex with some water and by the time we were near the hospital, the pain started getting better. The hospital knew I was on my way because Dave called ahead of time, so they had a cart waiting for me. They put a gown on me, started an IV, drew blood work, took an x-ray of my abdomen, gave me some medicine, and I felt completely better. The nurse said my potassium was low so she gave me a pill that was so large that I knew I would not be able to swallow it. I am not one to swallow pills unless they are small, so I told her that I could not swallow it. She ended up cutting it in half thinking it would help, but the rough edge of the pill didn't go down and I choked it back up. It still was too large for me to swallow so she ended up melting it in water and I was able to get it down that way. We were there for a little over an hour and I felt so much better. We still were scheduled for my mediport insertion within a few hours. Dave called Dr. Berri back and told him what happened, so he asked us if we wanted to schedule it the next day. I told Dave I didn't want to reschedule this procedure, so he didn't have to take another day off work. I knew we would have many doctors' appointments, tests, and I didn't want Dave to take off work unless it was necessary. We went home after we received the discharge paperwork to get a few hours of sleep. A few hours later we had to be at the other hospital in Detroit for my procedure. When we arrived at the hospital, we had to check into the surgical center. They took me back to a room where I was all by myself, so I was extremely anxious. The nurses were kind and supportive during the preparation for my procedure. They started an IV and soon I was taken back to the procedure room. I looked around and saw nothing but equipment, a table full of instruments, and huge lights over my head. All I remember before I was put to sleep was a nurse, who I thought was an angel sent from God, had the sweetest voice who told me that I would be fine. When I woke up, Dr. Berri and another doctor were there and told me everything went well. In the recovery room they monitored my vital signs and gave me some juice and crackers before I could go home. When I looked at my chest with my mediport in place, was a constant reminder of the cancer. Still, it felt strange to see this port protruding from my chest. I honestly did not feel it was there, so I wasn't too bothered by it. As a nurse, I was familiar with this IV access device, so I could understand the importance of having this in my chest. The port may affect people differently because of the body transformation and mental stigma that comes with it. I didn't let it bother me emotionally, but it was more difficult to process the whole situation. Thankfully, Dave was a doctor and helped me with all my medical questions and concerns.

The Importance of Family Support

I was so proud of my husband for being by my side through this but a part of me felt guilty. I don't like the feeling of being helpless or dependent. I am a strong-willed, outgoing, take-charge woman, who is used to serving her family, taking care of sick people in the hospital, and mentoring nursing students. I am so focused on others that sometimes forget I even exist. I felt guilty that my husband had to deal with his practice, our kids, his parents, and now my illness. He is a hero to me who gives so much of himself to everyone, and he is always in a good mood. I married him because I knew he was a Godly man, and I saw God working through him to handle everything with such ease. We have had our issues, arguments, don't always see eye to eye, but whenever I need him most, he is always there. Grandpa and grandma were also a blessing to me during my cancer journey They lived only five minutes from us, so we were able to assist them with their aging needs, but they in return helped us tremendously with our family needs. They helped with driving Joshua to and from school, meals, and support where needed. I was very weak from chemotherapy, so having grandma there to make the meals was a tremendous help. There were many days I couldn't lift my head off the couch and would tell the kids to visit grandma after school for dinner before they came home. Dave would stop there after work and bring the kids home. They were part of our family since we were married and having them living so close to us during this time assisted me to focus on healing. It came naturally that we would go to church together, grocery shopping, travel, and assist with projects around the house. I loved that my boys had such a special relationship with them, they were amazing role models, and were always there for their activities. The most important part of our lives that we shared, was our relationship with God. Being a Christian is never easy nor are we perfect in any shape or form. We struggle with sin and turn away from honoring God at times with our attitudes, behaviors, and expectations. What keeps us grounded is grace. Dave and I know that Jesus died on the cross for our sins and if Jesus can forgive us then we must forgive each other. I was able to face chemotherapy knowing God loved me, having a supportive spouse, and grandparents would carry me through the darkest days. God would lead me through this cancer journey, and I would grow in my faith to love Dave, his parents, and God more and more. With our faith in God and each other, we were ready to take on the next steps in the cancer journey.

The Process Leading up to Chemotherapy.

Before we started chemotherapy, we also had many more exams to complete. One of those tests was a PET scan. This scan, Positron Emission Tomography Scan, is a diagnostic examination used to diagnose diseases in the body by looking for areas of increased rate of chemical activities. My scan highlighted that there was increased activity in the sigmoid colon, liver, peri-aortic and iliac nodes. I'm not too fond of this or any type of scan because you must lay down on a hard table as they push you through a giant doughnut shaped machine. Before this test you must drink a barium drink and they inject you with a radioactive dye that helps the doctor detect exactly where the areas of cancer are. The next step was to biopsy my liver. Thankfully, the doctor who did this procedure put me at ease. Nothing is more frightening then having a probe being inserted into your liver, but they did give me a mild sedation to keep me calm. After the biopsy, I had to wait to be discharged for many hours while I laid in the recovery center. During this time, I started to feel some abdominal pain and cramping. The nurse told me to walk around, and it helped to relieve the gas pains. Eventually, they allowed me to leave when my vital signs were stable. The biopsy concluded it was the same cancer that was in my colon, so we had start chemotherapy as soon as possible. I was able to have all these procedures within two weeks which is a medical miracle. I always thank God for providing me with so many amazing doctors, nurses, and staff who assisted me along the way. It truly makes a difference when staff are kind, polite, and reassuring, because I was going through a lot of emotional turmoil.

Dave and I went together for my first chemotherapy treatment. I read a lot about the different medications that they were going to give me and tried not to focus on the side effects. I realized that everyone reacts differently by the same treatment because we are all individuals. I met with Patty when we arrived at the clinic. She worked with me at the hospital for many years, so I felt at ease knowing she was going to be my nurse. She always had a smile on her face, was a Godly woman, listened to me with understanding, and never left my side. She was instrumental in my progress, and I owe her a debt of gratitude for all she has done during this most difficult time. The chemotherapy medication would be administered through my mediport that Dr. Berri inserted. Remember that everyone is different, every cancer is treated with a specific regimen according to the oncologist, biopsy, tests results, and the patient's

The Process Leading up to Chemotherapy.

health care needs. I had many people question why I was getting the treatment I got because the person they knew was on a different treatment. All I could respond is that I'm not that person, and my doctor is treating me accordingly. Many treatments are similar but may vary according to the circumstances surrounding the cancer. Many people asked me why I wasn't on a certain experimental treatment, and I said we are just not there yet. According to my doctor, before we jump to experimental treatments, we must follow the guidelines stipulated by the Oncological Board of Medicine and the insurance company. The insurance company would not pay for experimental treatment until I failed all the available options that are a part of the standard of care. It was extremely difficult when people would tell me stories about their loved one dying from colon cancer or some other story that had nothing to do with my case. I believe it is best to not push your views on someone who is diagnosed with a terminal disease. What is more beneficial is just to ask how you can help or just tell them you will pray for them. People may believe they are being helpful, but it creates more stress when you must explain to them that you have it under control. I have asked my oncologist questions about some new treatment someone was adamant would help me. I was scheduled for 12 rounds of FOLFOX and Avastin for the next six months. We had no guarantee this would work, so the prayers and support were what kept me going. This was battle time for me as I knew this was going to be a war that would last a long time. When you go into a battle, you must obtain the best equipment necessary for you to endure and defeat the enemy. I was surrounded by an army, my family, and friends, who would battle with me. I put the armor of God on and looked to Him as my leader. My doctors were my generals who would help me with the strategy going forward. Dr. Wayne, my family doctor, was also instrumental in helping me with tremendous amounts of empathy and care. He always had great insight with different medications to help me tolerate the side effects of the treatment. One day, he told me that he bet I wished I could just sit on the sidelines and rest for a good amount of time. He was the one who told me I was running a race for my life, and he was so right. I couldn't stop battling, I was in a battle for my life, I had to stay the course, be strong, be positive, and do what I had to do until we changed battle plans or defeated the enemy. Cancer was the enemy that I was going to battle and defeat, because I was determined not to give up for "Losing is Not an Option!"

Battle Time

August of 2105, Dave, and I sat in the office for many hours as the nurse administered the chemotherapy. She started IV fluids through my mediport. We sat there patiently as she hung each drug when it was due. The environment was nothing to be excited about with the layout, small bathroom, and an older television to watch. I tried to take my medications given to me for nausea, but sometimes it just didn't work as quickly as I thought so I ended up heaving in the bathroom. This leaves you very weak and flushed feeling, so I would try to take sips of water. It was exceedingly difficult to try to swallow even sips of water without gagging. Sometimes it got so bad that I would end up taking an Ativan which is used to treat anxiety, but it would allow me to get some rest and end the cycle of nausea. The most challenging piece to all of this was I had three young children who relied on me as a mother. Thankfully, grandma was instrumental in assisting me with meals and people within the community brought us meals too. I believe grandma is the best cook in the world, but when I would come to the table, I was just too weak and had no appetite. My husband would encourage me to try to take a few bites, but I had no desire to eat. My brain was on overload thinking how I was going to handle the upcoming school year. What was most difficult was the chemotherapy pump I came home with for two days. It was part of the treatment program which made it frustrating to do much of anything with it around my waste with IV lines connecting to my mediport. I had to be extremely careful not to dislodge them from my port because the medication was toxic to touch with your bare hands. They gave me a special bag to put the medicine tubing and pump in if it ever became disconnected for any reason. They told me to clean up the spill with rubber gloves and dispose of them in the trash. This made me nervous until I got use to the process. On Thursday, I would go back to the clinic and the nurse would disconnect the pump until the next treatment, we would do this all over again. When she took that pump off, it felt so good, I was able to take a shower, and go about a normal lifestyle. The side effects of the chemotherapy would last a few days, but over a few more days, I would start to feel better just until starting the next treatment. The side effects seem to escalate over time with each treatment so I had to have a battle plan on how I would deal with this. Dr. Wayne was instrumental in helping me with this plan and it truly made a difference. The treatment made me start losing weight over time from the loss of appetite. I couldn't eat much of anything and lost my taste buds. I was starting to look fatigued, skinnier, and my hair was thinning out. The big issue with chemotherapy was alopecia, the loss of hair. My heart goes out to the women who lose their hair due to breast cancer, but my doctor said this treatment doesn't affect the hair follicles as much as the drugs used in breast cancer treatment. At first, I thought I would lose my hair, so I did go shopping for a wig. They are hot, uncomfortable, and they all look fake. The lady who assisted me had a private room where she assisted me with trying on each wig. She was such a blessing as she listened to my story and made me feel like a human being. The most difficult part of chemotherapy is feeling like you are a product being scanned and sent down the conveyer belt in the grocery store. People forget that you are a child of God, you have value, and you are worthy of being treated with dignity. This lady treated me with respect. Losing your hair can cause patients to become depressed, because their hair makes them unique from others. My hair didn't completely fall out, but over time, the texture, body, and amount of hair changed. It was hard for me to smile anymore because I felt so horrible inside and out. You can put a wig on and a ton of makeup to make you look good on the outside, but when you're going through chemotherapy, it destroys you emotionally. This is one of the reasons that makes this journey so difficult, and only God can lead you to a better place inside and out. Through a relationship with Jesus Christ, my savior, I was able to get through this challenge, because I knew He was with me all the way. I struggled with many questions that I pray about. All I know is that He loves me, I am His child, and His promise will be met when I am with Him forever in Heaven. His Grace is all I need in this world, and I looked at life with a totally different view. Nothing here on earth mattered to me except the people I loved the most, my family.

At the end of August, I had to take Joshua to orientation at his new school, Algonquin Middle School. I was not feeling all the best, especially carrying around the chemotherapy pump for everyone to see. I felt like a monster as everyone stared and questioned what was wrong. I had to explained to his teachers what happened with tears in my eyes and asked them to pay special attention to him just in case things go wrong. They were so special, and I couldn't be more happier knowing Joshua would have teachers who cared about all their students. They would be aware if he was struggling with watching me go through this cancer treatment. In fact, Joshua handled things better than I could have ever expected for a kid his age. He wrote poems in school for me that brought me to tears. At home he was always there to help me when I asked him for water while I was on the couch. The most special day was when I came home from my treatment and he laid blankets and pillows all over the couch, so I had a special place to rest when I came home. I just hugged him and sobbed, knowing that he had a heart for the Lord.

Battle Time

Joseph and Thomas were also instrumental in helping me through this difficult time. I asked them to be strong and to not allow their school studies to be interrupted by my cancer journey. This was an extremely busy year for us as Joseph was looking for colleges in his senior year while serving in the church, playing high school baseball and travel baseball too. Thomas was also busy with sports, travel baseball, confirmation, serving in the church, school, and social life. Joshua decided to put his talents and interest in music, so he played the trumpet, had weekday school, and assisted within the church. Somehow, we got through this with all my treatments, and I was able to even travel to many of the schools that Joe wished to attend. The boys not only maintained all A's, but stayed active in sports, church, and never got in any trouble. This gave me a piece of mind during my cancer journey. I didn't have to worry about my cancer and them falling apart too. I can credit their relationship with the Lord for this. They loved God and had a good heart, so they wanted to please their Father in Heaven, and their parents too. The rest of my treatments I had in the oncology office I would drive myself. Dave still had a full-time practice here in Algonac and as much as he loved me, he had to take care of many others who relied on his medical knowledge and advice. Dave is a well-respected family doctor and has practiced here for over 25 years. He delivered countless babies, and even sees patients at home. He stopped delivering babies many years ago, changed offices a few times, but is always willing to help others no matter who they are and where they came from. People would wonder why Jesus would sit with the most unholy people in His ministry, the tax collectors, the Samaritan woman, and so many who were thought to be unworthy. Jesus responded to them in such a dignified way, telling them that even the sick need a doctor too. He was telling them that people who are lost need a Savior and He ministered to their needs. Not everyone would listen to Jesus, but he gave them a choice to follow Him, or He would just move on. Dave treats people as Christ would want him to with dignity, honor, and respect. Dave shows our boys how to be servants of God in all they do.

One major issue I faced was the drop in my white blood cell counts and platelets to extremely low levels, so I had to skip a few treatments. Eventually, the doctor ordered a medication for my low white blood count. This medication was delivered through a tiny syringe underneath a disk attached to my arm, programed for a specific time. This new technology available is such a blessing for patients who can't get to the doctor's office for a shot. We were able to travel out of state with the medication disk attached to my arm. The medication disk would beep three times warning me that it was going to deliver the medication, I would feel a little prick in my arm, and I would then throw it away. This medication was called Neulasta, but I called it "Newblasta", because it made me feel extremely fatigued. You must maintain a sense of humor with your treatments, or you will spiral downward with depression. I struggled with depression on and off, but I made sure to take care of myself physically, emotionally, and spiritually. I also found that counseling was vital to hold me accountable, assist me with a plan to combat my depression, and talk with someone about my issues dealing with cancer. I did my best to eat a well-balance meal, drink plenty of fluids, and rest when needed. When visiting one of the colleges for Joseph and while we were talking with the coach, my pump went off. I don't know if he heard the pump beep, but I did and so did Dave. We just carried on like nothing ever happened. I have learned to tolerate many issues from my treatment along the way, that gave us something to laugh about later. The side effects were most difficult when we had to travel but I had to get through it. It wasn't easy, especially in the cold weather but I had to support Joseph in finding a college that he would be happy at. Everything depended on scholarship money, cost of the college, a good engineering school, and a baseball program that he would be accepted into. I had to be strong for Joe, so I made sure to surround myself with people who supported me and gave me tremendous amount of love. I believe that my spiritual journey is what kept me upbeat most of the times. I had an army of people at my church praying for me, sending me cards, listening to me, so between my pastor, deacon, and all the support I received at church, I was filled with the love of God. My relationship with Christ was the most important factor in this journey, even more important than chemotherapy. Christ is the way, the truth, and the light. He showed me so much love through the blessings along the way that I couldn't fall apart. People always wondered how I stayed so strong, and I always pointed them to God not me. I told them that it was God who is in me and holding me up with His love. He has a plan, and I would trust Him with my life even if it meant that it was time for me to come home. I believe that is the biggest fear people must struggle with but knowing I would be with Him forever gave me hope. By February of 2016, I had battled through 12 difficult treatments of chemotherapy. We would then meet with the doctor to discuss the next steps would be. My next step was to have another PET scan to see if the chemotherapy made any changes in the tumors that were there. By the grace of God most of the tumors shrunk to a significant degree. This was a complete miracle of God to see that this treatment worked so well. I had won the first battle, but the war raged on. Our next plan was deciding what to do with the colon and the tumors that were left in the liver. We discussed this plan with Dr. Kahn, and he sent me to a colorectal cancer specialist, Dr. Alame.

Colon Resection

After our discussion with Dr. Alame, we decided that he would be the physician to do a colon resection surgery. Before the surgery we had to have another colonoscopy, because the first one was never complete. The scope couldn't reach pass the tumor to see if there was anything else to be concerned about, so we had to repeat this procedure. By March of 2016, the kids were in the middle of school, sports, and Joseph was getting ready for college. We were busy, and I still was recovering from the first round of chemotherapy treatment. I lost almost 20 pounds, looked weak, my hair was thinner, still I pushed myself to stay strong for my family. Having another colonoscopy didn't bother me too much because I knew what to expect. The only thing I didn't enjoy was the prep before the scope, but I knew I was in good hands. Dave took me to the hospital, and after the procedure, the doctor was pleased to tell us that there was no further disease outside of the sigmoid colon which was extremely good news.

Sigmoid Resection

Dr. Alame said that the next step was to take out the cancerous section of the sigmoid colon and reconnect it so if there were cancerous cells there, they would not spread further. I was saddened to hear I had to have a surgery after everything I went through, but I trusted God would get me through it. The biggest concern for this procedure was that if he couldn't reattach it, I would have to live with an ostomy. An ostomy is an opening in the abdominal wall for stool to gather into a pouch outside of the body instead of going into the rectum. It would have a special bag attached to hold the stool and be emptied from time to time. This was not something I looked forward to, and even as a nurse I found it difficult to see someone with this. I put it in God's hands and prayed that the surgery would go well. While the kids were in school, I had my surgery. It's hard to remember everything you go through with how much stress I was under, but I do remember waiting in the pre-op room for some time. I just sat there thinking what my family was doing as I watched people being wheeled in and out of the area. The nurse had started my IV and I felt like it was eternity before it was my turn to be wheeled back. I remember being wheeled through the doors then the sedation hit me, and I don't remember anything after that. We found out later that the Dr. Alame almost didn't make it to do the surgery because he got stuck on his plane that was delayed from a conference in Texas. Dr. Berri would also be in the OR that day to look at my liver and had to cut his conference in Chicago short to be there. Dr. Alame did the resection, but while he was doing the surgery, Dr. Berri would look at my liver through the probe to see what was going on. Fortunately for me, both made it to do my surgery and did a fantastic job. Dr. Berri came out of the OR first and talked with Dave while I was in the recovery room. He told him that he saw a few tumors on the liver that will need to be followed up on in the future. He spent time talking to Dave about his ideas and the need for us to follow up with him. Then Dr. Alame came out and talked to Dave too. He told him everything went well, and he could see me when I got to my room. The best part of it all was I didn't need an ostomy! In fact, the surgery was done laparoscopy with only two insertion sites. I literally had two band aids on when I woke up. He was able to take off the cancerous portion and re-connect my colon. It was another miracle sent to me by God. As soon as the sedation wore off, I was in significant pain. I remember Dave at the bedside, my kids, my sister Liz, her husband Gus, and their two kids, Nina, and Gus. Dave had to leave that

Sigmoid Resection

night to take his state board examination. He stayed overnight at a hotel and took his examination the next day. Dave is a true hero for being able to manage all of this and I couldn't be prouder of him that he passed his boards with flying colors. The next day my neighbors, Chris and Jackie came to visit, our friends Steve and Cindy came the following day, and grandma came on Sunday, the day before I was discharged. My pain level was high, and the nurse gave me pain medication when I needed it. I do remember having a clear liquid diet on the second day and wanting another cup of coffee for Dave and me. What was upsetting was it took 20 minutes for the lady to bring me the coffee and she forgot to bring one for Dave. We had a few good laughs later from this experience, but at the time we were a bit frustrated. I was able to get out of bed within a short period of time, but the gas pains were so awful, I was buckled over in pain. Finally, one amazing nurse helped me to get the right medication and the pain went away. You cannot just take pain medication for gas pains; you must have medication to break up the gas and she was clever enough to get me this medication. I was supposed to go home within a few days but because I was in so much pain the doctor let me stay one more day. It worked out for the best because I do remember how much it snowed, and I didn't want to risk driving home in the bad weather. Fortunately, it was spring break for my kids, so they were all home and were able to visit me in the hospital. I felt bad for them because most of their friends were in Florida or somewhere having fun while they were stuck home. Life can teach us valuable lessons through tough experiences, and this was one of those times my kids had to learn that life was not all about them. We learned through this journey to trust in God, rely on each other, and life can send you a few curve balls along the way. Their faith in God was what truly opened their heart because they knew that they're here to be servants of the Lord, not to be self-serving. They didn't complain about not being able to go on vacation and were more worried about me. We had many vacations over the years where we had tons of fun, so missing one vacation was not going to be the end of the world. Besides, I would always remind them of families less fortunate than us who could not afford to go on vacation let alone had food, clothes, or much of anything else. We were Blessed with so much love that I didn't put much emphasis on materialism when I raised the kids. I was always giving things to charity and helping others who were less fortunate. Everything we have comes from the Lord, so I am thankful for everything and don't take things for granted. I was Blessed to be alive after that surgery, and I was thankful to be home with my family upon discharge.

Recovery from Surgery

I had to take the next few weeks to recover because soon I would have to face another round of chemotherapy. I still had a few tumors in my liver so we would have to look at options to treat those tumors too. All I knew was how grateful I was to be back home with my family. I couldn't process what was going to happen next. All I focused on was what I had before me, so I didn't become overwhelmed by the process. I had to recover and get stronger because I had a hard battle ahead of me. If I would have known everything I had to go through, I probably would have given up, but I focused on one thing at a time, and my faith in God led me each step of the way. The boys were back playing baseball again. It was Joseph's senior year and I loved watching him play. Thomas played junior varsity but was allowed to pitch one inning during a varsity game in Alpena. They both were pitchers and helped the team win many games with their skills. We had so much fun watching them play sitting in the stands. Dave was always in the dugout as one of the assistant coaches. Playing sports is a huge commitment between practices, all the games, traveling to different schools, and the traveling to tournaments on the weekends. Our days were filled with two boys who were extremely busy, and Dave had to juggle it all. I tried to go to most of their games despite feeling the effects from the treatment and surgery. Joshua didn't like to go to any of the games, so he would spend his time with grandpa and grandma. I didn't want to drag him to each game just to be miserable when he had so much fun being spoiled with grandpa's war stories and grandma's cooking. Joshua loved history and was a sponge learning from grandpa's stories. It's hard as a mom spreading yourself so thin between three active boys, but somehow, we did it. We made it through the high school baseball season with both boys and went directly into travel baseball next. Joe was getting ready to graduate soon and I was planning his graduation party. I wanted it to be the best party ever because I didn't know what the future was going to be for me. I loved my boys with all my heart and wanted to show them how much they were loved by being strong during this time.

Changing the Chemotherapy Treatment

My battle with cancer carried on, but so did life. Thankfully, my kids still were able to enjoy life, school, church activities, sports, and friends. The weather was starting to peak with warmer days filled with sunshine, so that made it even better. I love May because I get to plant my flowers just after Mother's Day when I know the frost will not kill them. We had so many things to prepare for, especially Joe's graduation. I had to plan a huge party, get signs, pictures, invitations, food, and the house ready for this event. We also had to visit again with Dr. Berri and Dr. Kahn so we can discuss the next step. They didn't want me to go without chemotherapy for too long so the tumors wouldn't start spreading again. I was maxed out on the FOLFOX regimen, so he decided to start me on FOLFIRI with Avastin because of the neuropathy I was experiencing in my feet. He also said that this drug was the sister drug and still would be part of the recommended treatment option according to the American Oncology Association protocols. We then discussed with Dr. Berri different options he could do to treat the tumors in my liver. He didn't want to put me through another major surgery at this point and thought it was too risky. His treatment plan consisted of removing half of my liver, allowing it to grow back, then go back to remove the other half. He said that sometimes cancer can still exist in tissues at the cellular level, but it is not visible until it is detected on the PET scan. He didn't want to risk this major of a surgery unless he had the equipment, team he needed, and felt it was too risky to proceed. He set me up to see a top surgeon, Dr. Knoll, at the University of Michigan Hospital. He wanted Dr. Knoll's opinion in what we should do next, but I would continue my chemotherapy treatment until August before continuing with surgery. The treatment would be stopped for a few weeks before having the surgery.

Graduation 2016

While we waited to see this doctor, life continued for the family. Joe graduated in the top 10 of his class and was well prepared for college. He decided to attend Illinois Institute of Technology in Chicago. He was accepted into their Chemical Engineer Program and on the Scarlet Hawks Baseball Team. The day of his graduation was extremely hot and humid. It was held in the back of the school on the football field, so we had to sit in the bleachers. It was a special time to honor all the kids, very emotional for the parents, and a day of joy for everyone. Joe's graduation party was just as exciting too, but it was extremely hot and humid on that day. Many of the people who came gathered in the house to stay cool, but nobody stayed too long and left after they ate. I had a catered chicken dinner with mostaccioli, macaroni and cheese, corn, salad, and dessert. The people who came didn't leave hungry and everyone had a good time. It was a lot of work setting up tents outside, preparing food, and making the house look special for Joe, but he was worth it. I wanted to make this his special day for being such an honorable young man. He never gave me trouble, he always did his best, and he was always there to support me. We had so many families and friends come that I was overwhelmed with emotions to see people that I haven't seen in such a long time. Memories flooded my mind as more and more people came. We shared so many stories about him growing up, some were very funny, and some were just about how great of a kid he was. The day sure went by quickly and before we knew it, it was time to start putting all the food away, put away all the tables and chairs, take down the tents, and clean up the messes. The best part of this was remembering asking Dr. Kahn if I would be there for Joe's graduation. By God's power and glory, I survived and was able to see my son graduate. Fortunately, I wasn't too sick from the side effects of the treatment because I took a week off chemotherapy.

At least I had two more years before Thomas would graduate so I had time to prepare. Thomas was a sophomore in high school and Joshua was in the sixth grade. What was going to be special is Joshua and Thomas would be in the same high school the following year because they consolidated the middle school and made the high school seventh through 12th grade. What was going to be special was Thomas would be driving Joshua to school, so I was off the hook with driving him. Thomas is an amazing person and assisted me with driving Joshua to many activities when I was not well. He had a part time job after school, working for a lady who assisted the school with uniforms. He made some money that he saved for his future college journey. Thomas wants to become a physician like his dad, so he was going to need to save a lot of money for college and medical school. He is a bright young man so I knew he would also obtain an academic scholarship. As a family we believed in working hard and giving back to the community. Part of giving back was the Hindy Strong Scholarship.

Hindy Strong Scholarship

When I was first diagnosed in 2015, the football team all got together to raise money for our family. One day all the coaches came over with a signed football from all the players and presented it to me along with a check from a community fundraiser. This touched my heart more than they could possibly know. Dave, Thomas, and I volunteered on the side lines to help injured players. Dave would run out on the field if a player got hurt to evaluate if there was a need to go to the hospital. We have treated many concussions, bruises, sprains, fractures, and broken bones over the years. The football team was doing quite well and ended up in the state semi-finals the following year. It was a cold snowy day, and we took a charter bus with some family friends and community members. It was a long drive to Battle Creek, so it was beneficial for us to travel together for safety reasons. Besides, it was a huge, warm, and comfortable bus that allowed us to have a good time celebrating our boys together on the ride there. We brought food and drinks for the long ride which made it even better. By the time we got there, it was snowing heavily. The coach was kind enough to arrange for me to sit in the press room while Dave and Thomas were on the sidelines. We had many injuries that day due to the cold weather. The boys were freezing, hurting, and giving so much for our community. The game was a battle to the end, but sadly we didn't win. I was freezing in the press room despite being dressed in multiple layers. The lady who arranged the bus trip for all of us had hot chocolate waiting for us when we got back aboard. I waited patiently for Dave, Thomas, and the rest of the people on our bus to come back. Everyone was extremely cold, tired, and disappointed with the loss. Our community is a small one in which everyone knows each other. Even the fire department comes to each game and honks the horn for each touchdown. The police, fire department, and all the parents would meet the boys on the way home during many games. This was such a great experience to be a part of and it just made me proud that we can help in any way we could for our school, the teachers, the students, and our community. We had so many amazing experiences with the team of players. My boys never played football, but they were always at the games. The stands were always packed in the student section with kids who cheered the team on. The parents would pack the other stands, the cheerleaders would give us a spectacular show, and with that much support, the boys could only be successful. I loved watching the boys play each game with such heart and determination to win. They inspired me during my treatment to have a no quitting attitude. I watched them pour their heart out each game, get hurt, and still go back out there with a winning spirit. I could feel the passion for the game, brotherhood, and spirit for victory. This inspired me to continue my treatment with courage. I was not going to sulk or be defeated with what I had to face. I was going to be a victor not a victim. Dave and I felt a special bond with the boys and appreciated their kindness during my cancer journey. I was so appreciative of them signing the football and giving it to me that I ended up framing it. The money they raised was more than we needed, and I honestly didn't want to take it from people who had little to nothing, yet they gave from their hearts. I felt deep in my heart that I wanted to somehow show everyone just what their friendship, prayers, and support meant to me. I prayed about it and decided that I would give the money back and ended up doubling it to start the Hindy Strong Scholarship the year of Joseph's graduation. I awarded six students with this award that year and I would continue to award students each year to come. I felt so proud to stand before the school and give a short speech to what the scholarship was about and how grateful I was for the community providing me with such love and support. People had tears in their eyes after I made my speech because it was filled with emotion, passion, and gratitude. I honored the students and stated why I felt they were honored to be given my scholarship that year. When you give back the Blessings you've received, I believe those people you touch will eventually make this world a better place. If everyone does their part to help others, this world would be such a great place to live in. I know I can't change the world, but if I can change one life at a time, then I believe I did my part to pass on a Blessing. God works through everyday people to make this world beautiful. There is evil in this world, but if we all did our part to shine God's light, I believe we can squash evil with good. Life is not always fair and bad things do happen, but if we can all come together as God would want us to, we can do far better than we can imagine. The Hindy Strong Scholarship was all about not giving up and helping students to succeed. I wanted to inspire the students to stay the course, have a vision, and keep going strong, Hindy Strong! If I could send this message, then going through cancer would not bring me down, but only uplift me. I want students to know that I believed in them, I would assist them, and I would always be there for them. I wanted them to know that they can't give up in life, maintain a spirit of optimism, and a winning attitude. The most important life lesson I wanted them to learn was, "Losing Is Not an Option"! I wanted them to go forward conquering the world making all their dreams come true.

God is our Foundation

God is the center of our lives through this journey, and our church plays a major role in guiding us in knowing just how much Jesus loves us. After cancer, illness, or a tragedy, many people will be angry at God, asking why did He allow this to happen to me? Why did He let my loved one dye? Why is there so much evil in this world? Honestly, I can't answer all the "why" questions and tell you everything is going to be just fine, or I would be lying to you. I'm not a Biblical scholar, pastor, priest, or anyone in authority to tell you more than I know. I don't pretend to have all the answers, and I don't want to give you false promises. The only thing I can tell you from scripture is that Jesus loves you, and if you believe in Him with all your heart, you will be in Heaven for eternity. We don't do good works to get to Heaven, we do good works because we want to please God and in response to what He did on the cross for us. Jesus was the perfect sacrifice and was obedient to the Father until the end. We are not perfect like Jesus, but we try to be obedient and follow His commandments. You may wonder, how can I be imperfect and flawed

Loving God: Living with Cancer

and still go to Heaven, the answer is Grace. God knows we aren't perfect, but He sent us His son to die on the cross to take away our sins. He paid the price, so we don't have to. If we repent of our sins, and ask God to come into our hearts, He will forgive our sins and welcome us into eternity with Him in Heaven. Remember the thief on the cross before Jesus died. Jesus told him that he would be with Him in Paradise. Jesus forgave a man in his dying hour because he was sorry for his sins and recognized Jesus as a Savior. Jesus can forgive you when you repent of your sins. My goal as a parent was to bring my kids up to know God and Dave shared that belief. We both loved God, worshiped together, prayed together, and were active in the church. We sent our kids to Immanuel Lutheran Pre-School during their earlier years of education before we sent them to kindergarten in the public school. We felt that this would give them a good foundation because the public school does not allow kids to pray or be taught about Jesus. We also sent our kids to Sunday school to learn lessons about Jesus. Dave and I were actively involved in teaching the kids these lessons. We believe that when you teach your kids about the Lord that this would honor God and help us to grow in our faith. We were also incredibly involved in weekday school with the kids. Every Wednesday, the kids would gather after school to learn about Jesus and enjoy a fun activity. This went on for many years until they were old enough to confess their faith upon confirmation. Confirmation classes were an extension of weekday school but were for the older kids. In the eighth grade, they would make their confirmation affirmed before the congregation. I assisted with being a table guide during the confirmation classes. I don't know if my boys appreciated me there because it was a time where kids felt free to discuss issues in their lives. Although, my kids were free at home to discuss any issues that bothered them, and we did not make them feel shameful for telling us. We always talked to our kids openly about life choices, temptation, and sin. We prepared our kids to understand that being popular is extremely important to many kids so they will follow the crowd and do things that we do not approve of according to our beliefs. We taught our kids to be leaders in the world, not followers, but to be followers of Christ. They realized it was not going to be easy standing alone for their faith, but they would have God's approval and ours. After years of learning about their faith in God, their hearts grew to know Him, love Him, and want to follow Him. We knew that they would stumble and rebel, but they always were sorry, and we always forgave them. We understand kids are not going to be perfect, we are not either. The most important lesson is to change your heart, change your ways, and ask God for forgiveness. All three boys served in our church in some capacity and were good leaders to other kids. They also were great witnesses to the kids in the public school who may not have been taught anything about Jesus. They showed their friends love and acceptance as Jesus would have asked them to. They shared their faith and the love of Jesus, hoping others would accept Him in their hearts too. My boys loved Jesus with all their hearts and their faith has helped them to deal with my cancer journey. They would pray and ask God for help in dealing with the ups and downs over the years. I'm sure this was not easy on them to watch their mother struggle with this disease and all the side effects that came with chemotherapy. They all filled my heart with joy when I was not well. They would bring me water, my medicine, but the one thing that filled me with joy was their hugs and kisses. Nothing heals a spirit more than the love you get from your kids. I could get through anything knowing how much they love me and how much I love them. It was the love we had in our family and God that always gave me the strength to get through everything. I love my family and am ever so proud of each one of them for who they are. Each one of my children are different in their own special way, but they all bring me great joy. My husband is a pillar of strength who assists me with bringing them up to be honorable young men. I honor my husband and hold him in my heart to be a man of honor, a Godly leader, and a wonderful husband. I am truly Blessed to have such a beautiful family so I would continue to do whatever I had to do in my cancer journey.

Understanding a Patient's Journey

By August 2016, I completed six rounds of FOLFIRI/Avastin chemotherapy treatment. I was trying to stay positive, but my energy level was wavering. Chemotherapy takes so much out of you with the ups and downs both physically and emotionally. Doctors, nurses, and everyone need to understand that you don't live with the disease but the emotional journey too. Chemotherapy weakens your body along with your mental, emotional, and psychological state of being. You have days where you are not as sharp to process your thoughts. You may be talking to someone and forget the words, ideas, or names of people in the discussion. This makes you feel embarrassed and frustrated. It also creates increased stress levels when in a public setting. You don't want to be in a situation where you forget someone's name or have a difficult time discussing an issue without feeling shame, guilt, or frustration. They refer to this as "chemo brain" to joke around, but sometimes it's just not funny. This happened to me often during conversations with people and I would feel embarrassed. I had a difficult time remembering things because I just didn't feel good, I was fatigued, nauseated, and in pain. The treatment took a toll on me with each round of chemotherapy I would receive. I would love to stop the treatment and give my body a break, but this was not up for discussion with the doctor. I had to continue my treatments even though my body, mind, and emotions were not up to speed. It creates increased emotional and psychological distress within your being when you are already feeling the side effects of the chemotherapy. Some people will even try to avoid putting themselves in situations where they must engage in group discussions. Now I can relate to many of my patients that I took care of more than ever before. I now understand why they were grumpy, short tempered, and non-compliant. They probably got to a breaking point where they lost all their coping skills. Many nurses become intolerant of patients like this when all they need is some compassion, understanding, and patience. People who are coping with a long-term illness lose their ability to cope and may need psychological help or medications to combat depression. I was extremely fortunate to have the best nurses who cared for me both physically and emotionally. They were so kind and understanding when I was not myself. They always listened to me tell them my fears, frustrations, and inner most hurts. They showed me love and support during each treatment that I was more than thankful. They saved me from giving up hope and I was able to continue my treatment with success. There are far more obstacles that a cancer patient faces beyond the mental, emotional, and physical. There are financial issues to deal with when the insurance company or hospital billing fails to cover a treatment. You can end up spending hours on the phone trying to deal with these issues. Before each treatment, you must get your blood drawn so they know it's safe to administer the chemotherapy. There is stress when your laboratory values are not within normal limits, and you cannot get your treatment. This makes you feel let down and fearful that something traumatic will happen as a result. The day of your treatment takes many hours to complete, so patience is a necessity to endure the time it takes out of your day. It also takes time to drive back and forth to the clinic where they administer your treatment, so this too can add stress, especially if you get stuck in traffic. There were times where I would have to go to another clinic to get my treatment, and this was incredibly stressful on me because I don't like to drive far. Then after the treatment, you're not feeling well, and you must drive all the way home. Some days when I left the clinic, I was nauseated so I made sure to bring a water bottle to sip on as I drove home. There are so many obstacles in addition to the treatment that people must face which makes everything more difficult to endure. When I would get home, I still had to take care of my family with daily chores. I had places to go with the kids, shopping, cooking, cleaning, and the day-to-day things to do as a mom. Then there were days I was not well enough to accomplish anything, so I had to ask for help. Asking for help was difficult for me because I felt like a failure as a mom. This was a very unrealistic expectation of myself, but I was used to being a highly active, energetic mom. It was hard enough to give up my career as a nurse and educator, but to not be able to take care of my kids the way I was used to was emotionally difficult for me. I love my kids and I always gave so much of my time and energy to care for them, so anything less made me feel defeated. This stress can make or break you; it can change the course of how you face your disease, and it can also be detrimental in the outcome. Fortunately, for me, this stress was relieved by my family and faith. My boys were amazing at being independent, responsible, and assisted me with things I couldn't get done. They learned this from the team spirit of sports, stepping up and being a team player. Dave was amazing too with doing his best to help me with things around the house. He wasn't the kind of husband to come home from work, flop on the couch, and expect to be served because he worked all day. He was the leader of our home who would always pitch in where was needed and he did it with a cheerful heart. My cancer journey was made easier because of the love and support I received. I believe that God was holding me up with His love through the people in my life. My faith was instrumental in my healing, my physical and mental health, and my strength and endurance.

I spent more time praying and getting to know God during this trial, and I learned that I am totally dependent on His Grace. I had tremendous support from my church family who prayed for me. I believe prayers are heard and God gives us what we need to get through the darkness by being the light at the end of the journey. I knew that His love was what carried me through the darkest days. You may believe you can't get through another minute, hour, our day with cancer, but with God, he turns the "I can't" into "I can".

I am in a Dark Place

Everyone who is going through a terminal illness has their own story, so I don't want to sugar coat mine. Everyone is experiencing their own thoughts, side effects to their treatment, financial stress, emotional struggles, and spiritual battles. I do not want to diminish anyone who is reading this or sound like I am lessening their pain. I can't tell you that being a Christian is going to make it all better. I can't tell you there will be a cure or healing. I won't say anything that will give you false hope. I cannot tell you how to think, what to believe, or how you should process all of this. My prayer is that you know or come to know that God loves you, your sins are forgiven, and that you are not alone in your journey. I can't assume everyone reading this is a Christian, but I pray that you can find hope in Jesus Christ as your personal savior. I believe in God and in my heart, I know that my relationship with Him has assisted in pushing myself farther than I ever thought possible. You may not know Jesus or may not even want to discuss this at this time. All I can do is pray for you to seek Him at some point. A relationship with

Loving God: Living with Cancer

Jesus is not about feeling good all the time, it's not about what you get from Him, but what you give of yourself. Now, you're probably saying that I am out of my mind because you have nothing more to give. I can respectfully disagree with you and speak, "yes, you do". When we give of ourselves, we receive so much in return. Giving doesn't have to mean financially, physically, or something that you're not capable of doing because of your illness. Giving may be as simple as showing kindness to the nurse who is caring for you, a smile to your loved one, or listening to someone in distress. I believe everyone has a gift of giving, and even though you may be suffering or physically incapable of giving, you can give a gift from your heart. I believe Jesus gives everyone the opportunity to reach out to touch others. I'm writing this book so I can give people a better understanding of what it is like to battle cancer. I couldn't have done this without knowing Jesus Christ and spending time getting to know Him better. I am at peace knowing that if I do die, I will be going to Heaven to spend eternity with Him. This gives my family great comfort knowing that someday we will all be together again. Jesus gives me my daily needs just like it says in the prayer, "Our Father". "Our Father", is God who is the most loving God you will ever know once you take the time to get to know Him through prayer, Bible study, going to church, and fellowshipping with other believers. "Who Art in Heaven" is where God is and He wants a relationship with you so you can be with Him forever.

I am in a Dark Place

"Hallow Be Thy Name." We refer to God as Holy and His name should never be taken in vain like so many people do today. His name should never be used in a curse word or in any sentence that distains his Holiness. "Thy Kingdom Come, Thy Will be done on Earth as it is in Heaven." He gives us the Holy Spirit who is with us daily. His will is done when He strengthens us to overcome evil, and one day all evil will be defeated, then we will spend eternity with God. There is only one way to get to Heaven and that is through Jesus Christ. "Give Us This Day Our Daily Bread and Forgive Us for Our Trespasses as We Forgive Those Who Trespass Against Us." God gives you everything you need here on earth, and He will forgive you when you mess up. We need to forgive others too when they hurt us. We must remember that everything comes from God. So many people work their whole lives for money, possessions, and things that will not make a difference in the long run. Instead of idolizing all your money and possessions, being boastful, searching for more and more, it's best to praise God for what you do have. When you use your gifts to help others then you will find yourself in a better place, if you do it for God's glory and not your own. The prayer also says to "Lead Us Not into Temptation but Deliver Us from Evil." God is there, so we do not get tempted by things here on earth. God doesn't tempt us, but He guards our hearts, soul and mind so that we can resist the devil. Therefore, it is so important to stay in the Word of the Bible, go to church, pray, fellowship with other believers, and repent when you mess up. "Deliver Us from Evil." He saves us from every evil. "For Thine is the Kingdom and the Power and the Glory Forever and Ever, Amen." Jesus said to his disciples that there are only two basic commandments that summarize everything, "Love God with All of Your Heart, and Love Others." This prayer has helped me with the darkness. I have been in a dark place many times. I have cried my eyes out, been angry, hurt, frustrated, discouraged, and so many other emotions that kept me from seeing the light of God. Sometimes people are just not there yet, they must process their emotions, they must get through the rough days physically, mentally, emotionally, and spiritually. This doesn't happen overnight, and everyone does it in their own way. My only advice is that you cannot stay in the dark for too long or the disease will get the best of you. There must be a time where you seek professional or spiritual help to assist you in coping with your disease. You are not going to be feeling like jumping up and down praising Jesus during those dark days. You might even have times where you are angry at Him because you don't feel His presence; and that is okay. You might go through a period of denial about your illness and not seek treatment. This is an extremely dangerous place to be in mentally because it could mean the difference between life and death. When someone is in denial is the most heartbreaking moment the loved ones will go through. I remember when my mom was diagnosed

I am in a Dark Place

with breast cancer, and she did not believe she had it. This hurt me deeply because I did not want to see her suffer and die. This was a huge reason why I became a nurse. I wanted to be an advocate for people suffering with a disease. I wanted to educate people about their disease. I wanted to assist in counseling family members through the challenges of watching a loved one suffer. This is not the time for blaming, shaming, or getting angry at someone when they're in the dark. It is time to walk beside them, support them with encouragement, help them with their fears and anxieties, and discuss their needs. People react very differently during diagnosis or treatment stages. For many, it is hard to find a light outside the dark tunnel, and it takes time to get them through the darkness to the light. I was touched by the support I received. People at my church pray for me. When I attend service, I have so many people come up to me and show me love and support that it totally changes my focus and mood. I have people in my community, friends, neighbors, and my family who show me unconditional love and support. This gives me the confidence to get through each round of chemotherapy, surgery, test, or whatever I must face next. I may be in a dark place for a moment or two, but I always seem to come to a better place with God and my support system by my side. I will honor Him in this journey by being a witness to His Glory. I will do this by showing people there is a way out of the darkness, but they must trust God, they must know God, and they must be obedient to God. God will be there through the journey shining the light even in the darkest moment with His love. Even when it's hard to see, you don't have to be in the dark if you just give it to God. Allow Him in your life and heart and let Him lead the way. You will never go wrong because He is the Way, the Truth, and the Light forever and ever more. There is so much fear that keeps you in the dark, but God takes away your fear when you have faith in Him. With God you can overcome and persevere during the most difficult days, and He will pave the way to a better place of hope, peace, and love. Please don't give up hope, for God loves you and He will never let you go, trust Him, He is an Awesome God!

Preparing for Another Surgery

It was time to decide the next option for the tumors that still existed in my liver. By the grace of God, all my tumors were gone but the ones in my liver. We decided to go back to discuss options with Dr. Berri. He leads a program called HIPEC (Hyperthermic Intraperitoneal Chemotherapy) that treats cancer that have spread to the abdominal cavity. We needed a team of experts to give us opinions and options. Having cancer is quite frightening but God sent us the right people to help us make the best decisions. We needed guidance, information, and options that would best fit my specific cancer needs. Many people compare their cancer to others who don't even have the same cancer. Even with the same cancer, you cannot compare because you are a unique human being with totally different DNA. I never try to tell people what to do for their cancer except to pray, seek information from the experts, and make informed decisions. Dr. Berri was so helpful and honest when we sat with him. He was so kind and compassionate to what I was going through as well. I was overwhelmed with everything I was reading on the internet. He told me to stop reading that stuff because I was not a statistic, and those studies were not current or accurate. What he wanted me to focus on was a good outcome. The biggest issue with my liver were the tumors located in both lobes. These tumors made surgery a difficult decision. The liver has two lobes. Dr. Berri was considering removing one lobe which would grow back over time, and later remove the second lobe. The dilemma with tumors is that sometimes doctors cannot see microscopic cells that are growing in the liver. However, as we talked further, we realized this would be a major surgery. After losing 20 pounds, all the chemotherapy I received, and still being quite weak, this was not the best option. He wanted me to discuss this further with an oncologist and surgeon at the University of Michigan Hospital in Ann Arbor. He referred me to see Dr. Krauss and Dr. Knol. Dr. Krauss is the Assistant Professor Director, Regional Oncology Services, Division of Hematology/Oncology Department of Internal Medicine. Dr. Knol is the Cyrenus G. Darlin, Sr. and Cyrenus G. Darling Jr. Professor of Surgery and a member of the Division of Gastrointestinal Surgery in the Section of General Surgery. The Cyrenus G. Darling Sr. and Cyrenus G. Darling Jr., M.D., is a Professorship in Surgery that honored his father and grandfather, so having these credentials tells us he is an outstanding surgeon who specializes in gastrointestinal surgery. Dr. Berri knew them

Preparing for Another Surgery

personally and set up the consultation with both. The struggle with any major hospital is that it takes time to get an appointment with a physician that takes patients from around the world. Thankfully, we were able to obtain an appointment on the same day with both doctors within just a few weeks. If you have ever been to a large hospital, the visit can be quite overwhelming, but they were awesome because they sent us a packet of information before our appointment. We had directions of where to go, where to park, and how to get to his office. As we approached the hospital, my heart sank in my stomach when I saw how enormous it was. I worked at a large hospital when I started my job in nursing, but this hospital made that one look quite small. The hospital stretched out for blocks; we were in awe the size of it. We were also thankful for having the opportunity to have this as an option. All I thought about was all the staff working there and how many lives they were saving. We were blessed to have skilled physicians trained to be part of such an elite hospital with an excellent reputation. I was nervous and unsure of what I was going to face as we entered the large parking structure and found a place to park. We looked at the map that they provided us and headed into the building to see exactly where to go. As we entered the building, we were greeted by a friendly lady at the front desk who directed us where to go from there. I looked around and saw so many ill people. Everyone was there for a different purpose but all of us were there because we had cancer. We were in the cancer center area of the hospital and were directed to Dr. Krauss's office. When we arrived, we were met by another friendly face who directed us to go down the hall to the check in area for the doctor. We stopped at the front desk and filled out paperwork for the doctor to look at. I made sure to fill out the paperwork in full so they would have all the information needed about me during the evaluation and treatment process. One suggestion I would provide for my patients and families is that it would be a great idea to have a record on hand with a list of all your current medications, surgeries, and treatments so that when you do go to the doctor or end up in the emergency room for some unforeseen reason, you can provide the professionals with the most up to date information. This allows them to administer lifesaving medications and treatments in a safe environment. I was not on any medications, but I provided them with a list of my treatments, surgeries, and medical history for me and my family. After filling out the paperwork, a nurse did the normal routine of weight, height, blood pressure, heart rate, temperature, and oxygen level. I was happy to see all the readings were within normal levels. Then she took us back to a room where we had to wait to see the doctor. Waiting is part of the package deal when you are scheduled to see a doctor, especially a busy one who works for the University of Michigan Hospital. I know too well from my own husband why doctors are always late, they're extremely busy. Dave gets pulled in so

Preparing for Another Surgery

many directions before he sees his next appointment. Sometimes he gets calls from the emergency room, the hospital, or a patient who has an urgent problem. We waited patiently for the doctor to enter the room and we were quite anxious for what he had to say. We both prayed together so we would make the right decision, we prayed for the doctor to find a way to remove the tumors with ease, and we prayed that this would be the last step in my cancer journey, even though we both knew it was not. When the doctor walked in the room, he introduced himself and asked me a lot of questions. He discussed my cancer diagnosis, progress, and different treatment options. He stated that he would collaborate with Dr. Kahn, my local oncologist, so if I needed further chemotherapy, I didn't have to travel all the way to Ann Arbor. It was a brief appointment because I had already received adequate chemotherapy treatment that had shrunk all the tumors except for the ones in my liver. He agreed that the next step would be to have the tumors surgically removed and was happy we had an appointment with his colleague, Dr. Knol. Our next stop was to see Dr. Knol. We checked in at the waiting area only to be given more paperwork to fill out. You must maintain a sense of humor when visiting two doctors in one day. I don't believe they share the same charts in their office, so yes, we had to fill out additional paperwork. We waited patiently again to be called back to have my vital signs checked and be taken to a room. We anxiously waited for the doctor to arrive, but when he did, we were pleased to meet him. He greeted us with a kind spirit, soft eyes, but he had a concerned look on his face. After a long discussion, we concluded that he would do a liver resection. He would remove the tumors that were left in my liver by resecting the ones that were there. He said within a few weeks my liver would re-grow new tissue in that area, but it would be a significant surgery. He planned on removing my gallbladder while he was there too, so if I ever had a gallbladder issue in the future, I wouldn't need another surgery. This man had my life in his hands. I had to give him all my trust. This is a huge decision to make with any surgery for anyone. I had a colon resection surgery before this, but this was much different. This surgery would take more time to complete, more time to heal, and it was very risky to do. I asked him if he's done this surgery before, and with a chuckle, he said yes. The man has done plenty of these surgeries and other major surgeries throughout his career, but I just felt I had to ask. I believe a better question would have been was, is this my best option? This was my best option because it didn't require me to have half of my liver removed. He felt that was too aggressive of an approach. After our discussion, he said he would set up the surgery and have his staff reach out to me when it was scheduled. We left the office feeling relieved but still very anxious of what was next. This is when you get down on your knees and ask God for mercy. This is the time when you really fear for your life and pray that this doctor will save it. I had to trust God would Bless this doctor to open my abdominal cavity and remove the tumors in my liver that were only centimeters long. It was all incredibly overwhelming. I knew this was going to take time to process. This was the time for prayer, asking God to shine His light on this. My faith in Christ is what got me this far, and it would be that faith that would guide me all the way to the end of my journey. All of this seemed unreal at times, as if I were having a bad dream. Here I am now facing yet another surgery after going through chemotherapy. I would have never pictured or factored this in my life being the planner that I am. I had it all figured out from the moment I said "I do" when I took my wedding vows. I was going to be a nurse, raise a family, my kids would go to college, get good jobs, have grandchildren, and life would be picture perfect. Then cancer entered the picture. Life doesn't always go the way you plan it, and I felt a great sense of disappointment being the control freak I was. I knew God had a plan no matter what the outcome was, and I would trust in Him that He would get me and my family through this surgery. All I could do now was wait.

Time for Surgery

Facing another surgery is no easy task. In fact, it comes with preparation both physically and emotionally. I was still recovering from many rounds of harsh chemotherapy, and I was emotionally spent. I felt as if I was climbing a mountain not knowing when I would get to the top, or was I going to slip off a cliff just to fall flat on my face. You are tired, you are down, you're all over the place with emotional grief. All I knew was this was a battle that I had to win, and I was not going to wave the white flag of defeat at this point. I was going to face my fears with God and go through the surgery the doctor recommended to save my life. Before I was scheduled for my surgery, the doctor recommended an MRI so he could look at the films to make sure there were no additional tumors hiding in my liver. Having an MRI for me was terrifying because I am extremely claustrophobic. I told my doctor this despite feeling shameful. He told me I could have sedation before the test which put me at ease. I was not even aware that this was an option, so you can see how important it is to discuss all your options with the doctor. Again, we had to drive all the way to the hospital in Ann Arbor and report to the MRI department. When I arrived there, we waited for them to take me back to a changing room to put a hospital gown on. After I changed, I sat there waiting in so much fear I almost had a panic attack not knowing what to expect. A nurse came and got me before too long. She took me back to a nursing station where she took my vital signs, started an IV, and discussed the process for the test. This nurse was extremely compassionate. She sat next to me and listened to my story as tears rolled down from my eyes. She was so kind with her words and showed me that she understood. If she were not so kind, I don't think I would have made it through this test without falling apart. Walking to the MRI room, we came through a large set of doors, and the machine looked enormous to me. I felt so small, it was overwhelming to be in that room with only a hospital gown on. A technician was there to help with the procedure. The room was cold, but the nurse provided me with a warm blanket when I laid on the table that would slide me back and forth into the machine. The nurse put oxygen on my face, strapped me in, and just before the technician slid me back into the large machine, the nurse injected me with a medication that made me fall asleep. I was totally relaxed, and the technician slowly moved me back into the machine. After a while, the technician moved me outside of the machine where I started to wake up. I was told the test was not over and before I was put back into the machine, the

Time for Surgery

nurse gave me another dose of the medication. Before I realized it, the test was done, and they assisted me off the cart. The nurse was still with me and directed me back to the nurse's station where she took my vital signs again and gave me some crackers and juice. When I was more awake, she said I could change and go home. I thanked her with a grateful heart. The next step was to wait for the doctor to read the report, look at the films, and schedule me for my surgery.

The day came when the staff called me to schedule me for my surgery. The nurse tried to obtain a consent over the phone but there was a problem with what she told me. You must pay attention to what you are consenting to before you agree to have a surgery. She stated the surgery correct but did not include that the doctor was going to remove my gallbladder at the time too. I informed her that the doctor discussed that with me. What I didn't appreciate was that she became argumentative and said that they don't normally do that with this surgery. I told her again that my doctor said he was planning on doing this, so she said that they would call me back. I was not going to give my consent for a surgery without having the gallbladder removal on the consent. Within an hour, the nurse called me back and said yes, she talked with the doctor, and he was planning on removing my gallbladder. I gave my consent but didn't appreciate her sarcasm. Patients are going through enough issues and don't need staff to be argumentative, rude, or sarcastic. You wonder why patients become intolerant of staff at times because they have reached their limit with everything they are going through. This was a total contrast to the kind nurse who assisted me with my MRI exam. They scheduled the surgery for a Friday which was perfect for Dave's schedule and Joe was able to take the Megabus that took him directly to a stop not too far from the hospital. The night before the surgery we arranged to stay at a Hampton Inn for the weekend. The hotel eliminated a two-hour car ride on the morning of the surgery. Besides, I wanted to be able to have a nice dinner with my family and a good night sleep. Thomas didn't come with us because he wanted to be with his friends at the high school football game that Friday night. Our friends from church brought him up the next day and he then stayed with Dave, Joshua, and Joseph in the hotel Saturday night. We got to the hotel with plenty of time to go out to dinner. We went to a local favorite restaurant called Zingerman's Roadhouse. We had to wait for a table because the place was so popular, and they were busy during the dinner rush. As I looked at the menu, I realized I didn't want to order a huge meal before my surgery the following morning. The waitress was so kind and assisted me with finding a good choice. Dave led us in prayer as we always do before a meal thanking God for our food. After dinner, we went back to the hotel, prayed together, and lounged in our room before falling asleep. Thankfully, we didn't have to get up too early because my surgery was scheduled for 10 a. m., and we didn't

Time for Surgery

have to get there until an hour before. Our plan to sleep in was changed when we got a call at 7 a. m. from the pre-op nurse who was wondering where we were. I told her that we were told our surgery was not scheduled until much later. She was very apologetic and told me there must have been a mistake in the operating room schedule, and to get there as soon as we could. What a shock to wake up to that call! When we got there, we went directly to the pre-op area, and they took me right in. I only had time for a quick hug and kiss goodbye to Dave and Joshua. They took me to a bed, closed the curtains, and gave me a gown to change into. Those gowns are thin, but they were kind enough to provide me with a heated blanket. The staff started my IV, took my vital signs, and I had many people come in and out to talk to me. Then two doctors came in to discuss my anesthesia and pain control options. This young doctor was especially kind explaining he wanted to insert an epidural catheter in my back to give me medicine that would numb me from chest down so I wouldn't feel pain before and after the surgery. He was extremely pleasant in his demeanor and said if it were his mother, he would recommend this catheter. He explained that I would have to sit on the side of the bed bent over while he inserted the catheter into my spinal cord. This made me quite concerned even as a nurse because I understood the complications that could have happened as a result. His explanation calmed my fears, so I consented to the procedure. He had another physician with him who helped him insert the catheter. They did an excellent job. I had absolutely no pain or discomfort. I was all prepped for surgery, and just before they wheeled me back to the operating room, an anesthesiologist gave me some medications in my IV to put me to sleep. The only thing I do remember is waking up with many staff members moving me into my bed in my room on the surgical floor. I was still quite groggy when Dave, Joshua, and the doctor were at my bedside. The doctor seemed quite happy with the surgery and after I asked him about the nasogastric tube being removed, he told the staff to remove it. I felt like a train wreck with IV tubing, nasogastric tube, oxygen tubing, a surgical drain from my incision site, a urine catheter, a sequential compression device on my lower legs to prevent blood clots, and I had over 20 staples from my right side under my ribs that wrapped all the way around my abdomen to the tip of my sternum. One thing I could say was the doctor who put the epidural for pain control in me was spot on, I was in no pain. I was so happy to see everyone upon returning to my room. My sister came with her husband and two kids, my husband, and Joshua made me feel at ease. Later that night, Dave and my brother-in-law, Gus, went to pick Joseph up from the bus station, and I couldn't have been happier to see his face when he arrived. I was quite sleepy after the surgery because of the anesthesia was still in my system, so I had a difficult time staying awake to talk with everyone. They didn't stay too long because they knew I needed my rest, so they all said their goodbyes and left. Dave took both Joseph and Joshua back to the hotel. I honestly do not remember much that happened that evening other than the nurses taking my vital signs often and checking on me. The next day Dave brought the boys to visit, and I was so excited when they came. Thomas came to see me that morning with two friends from our church. I was so thankful that they were kind enough to drive Thomas to come see me that morning. Joseph and Thomas left in the afternoon because Joseph's friend from college had tickets to a University of Michigan football game with his parents. It was exceedingly kind of his friend to invite the boys. I'm sure they would have been bored sitting around my small private room all day. Joshua didn't mind staying in my room because he had homework to complete and a new game came out, Civilization VI, so he spent the day playing on his computer. My sister came with her husband and two kids later in the afternoon, so it was nice for Joshua to spend time with his cousins. I had a busy morning because the nurse started to discontinue many of my tubes. She disconnected my IV, took my oxygen off, removed the sequential compression device, and wanted me to ambulate and sit in the chair. Dave assisted me to the chair which took some time to get situated with my urination catheter and surgical drain. The spinal epidural medication was discontinued when the doctors did their rounds, so I had to ask for pain medication. The nurse gave me pain medications before I got out of bed to sit in the chair for lunch.

I still felt quite out of it and was very weak but enjoyed the company. My sister didn't stay too long because she had to get back home. Dave stood by my side and assisted me in ambulating from the chair to the door. It took everything out of me to do that with my large surgical incision and being very weak after surgery. Eventually, he assisted me back to bed to rest. There's not much to do after you have a major surgery but visit with your family, talk to all the doctors who check on you, and try to ambulate as much as you can. Honestly, you start looking forward to when your food tray comes up because it breaks up the boredom for a moment. Hospital food is nothing special, but it gives you something to do while you're sitting there. The one thing that comforted me was having a warm cup of coffee with my trays. Everyone from the housekeeper, the food service workers, the doctors, and all the nurses were incredibly kind. My nurse made sure to ask me if I was in pain each time she came into the room and gave me pain medication as needed. I have a good pain tolerance and didn't ask for too much pain medication while I was there. The only time I was in horrible pain is when the nurse practitioner removed my drainage tube. She was talking to my husband while removing my drainage tube, her technique was far from gentle. She yanked that tube extremely hard and fast out which almost took my breath away. I was very upset after she did this, so I asked the nurse for pain medication. The nurse gave me two pain pills and I told her I only wanted one. This time the nurse seemed irritated with me because she made a snippy comment. Well, me being a nurse felt that was inappropriate. First, you don't get snippy with your patients, ever. Second, she never assessed my pain level when I asked her for pain medications. She assumed my pain level was extremely high and gave me two pain pills. Normally a nurse should ask for your pain level and ask you if you would prefer one or two pain pills. She didn't see on the chart I was only taking one pain pill each time I was given pain medications. I felt that two pain pills would make me too groggy, and I honestly thought that one pill would take the pain away. I also felt that if my pain were not relieved, I could always ask for more pain medication. I know most people do take two pills when given pain medications, but the order usually reads one to two pills as needed leaving it to the discretion between the nurse and the patient. The pain medication worked, and I eventually fell asleep. When I felt better, Dave helped me take a walk outside my room. I was thankful to be able to get out of bed and out of my room. I could only walk a short distance and had to come back. I thought it was a great idea that the hallway had labels on the wall with markings that measured out every 25 feet. This helped me measure how far I could walk. For my first venture, I was only able to walk just beyond my door and I had to come back to sit down. Later that day, I was able to walk up to 25 feet and back with Dave's help. I knew I was going to be there a few more days and I would be able to walk farther each day. When Joseph and Thomas came back from the game, it was getting late, so we had a short visit and Dave took them all back to the hotel for the night. I didn't like to be in the hospital all by myself, especially at night, I missed my family. I spent my time resting and watching television. The evening nurse came in and removed my urination catheter, so it was much easier to get up on my own with no tubes to fuss with. At this point, I was able to get out of bed myself, and sit in the chair. After the surgical drain was pulled, the nurse practitioner placed a dressing on my incision site, but later that evening I noticed it was saturated with blood. I was in the bathroom cleaning up and after I bent over to clean myself up, I noticed blood dripping all over the floor. I put on my light and when the nurse came in, she seemed quite startled to see so much blood. This didn't bother me the least after working over 15 years in the ICU, it happens. She helped me to clean up the blood with more towels, a doctor came to look at it, and he put a dressing over it. I had a feeling that the dressing he put on the site was not going to work, but I didn't want to tell him what to do. As a nurse, I would have put the patient back in bed, obtain a large, padded dressing, hold pressure until it stopped bleeding, and then apply a heavier dressing with surgical tape. As I was sitting back in my chair, I noticed the dressing was saturated with blood again, so my assessment was correct. This time the nurse assisted me back to bed, and when the doctor came, he said he would have to put some stiches in to

Time for Surgery

keep it from bleeding again. I was not thrilled with that option, but the doctor was gentle with his approach, so I felt safe. I laid flat in the bed on my side. It only took him a few minutes to put in a few stiches to stop the bleeding, and it worked. The nurse gave me my pain medications and I eventually fell asleep for the night. In the morning, the doctors came to see me, the nurse took my vital signs, and I was sitting up in the chair waiting for Dave and the boys to visit. I was still moving slow, but when we went for a walk outside my room, I was able to walk halfway down the hall and back. It was nice to see what was going on in the other rooms and it made me miss being a nurse. Dave had to take Thomas and Joshua back home that evening, Joe took the Megabus back to Chicago, they all had school on Monday. Only Dave would come visit me for the next few days. I was thankful for grandpa and grandma to help Dave with the kids while I was in the hospital. Grandma made all the meals for them, and grandpa drove Joshua to and from school. I was in the hospital until Wednesday. Each day I was able to walk a little further and was getting a bit stronger. The night before I was discharged, I was able to walk completely around the nurse's station and was immensely proud of my progress. Dave came to pick me up the morning of my discharge and I couldn't be more thankful to be going home. God did not leave me throughout the entire time in the hospital, so I looked up in the sky when we were on the road driving home and praised Him.

Recovering from Liver Resection Surgery

Recovering from liver wedge resection surgery was going to take some time and patience, but I was a mom. I wanted to be there for my kids. That evening we had to get ready for Joshua's band concert. Joshua did not play sports like the other boys; he was gifted in playing the trumpet. He also played the keyboard and piano. I always enjoyed hearing music in our home. Dave got a wheelchair from the office and had to wheel me into the gymnasium so I could attend. I felt embarrassed being wheeled in. It felt like everyone was staring at me. Thankfully, our community is small, and we know many people so most of them knew I had just gotten back from surgery. We all enjoyed the concert, and Joshua played his trumpet quite well. When we got home, I was not able to walk up any stairs, so I slept downstairs on the recliner. This was difficult for me, because I am an active person and was accustomed to sleeping in my bed. Although after sleeping in the hospital bed for so many days, I was thankful just to be home. I really missed my family, home, and good food. Hospital beds are not comfortable, your meals are bland, and you feel alone. Thank God for grandpa and grandma who helped me daily with the cooking, cleaning, and caring for the kids. The hospital doctors agreed that Dave could take out my staples, so I didn't have to drive two hours for them to remove them. I honestly felt more comfortable with Dave removing them because he would be gentler. My son Thomas was interested in becoming a physician, so he assisted his father in removing my staples. At this time, I was able to walk up the stairs slowly, so we took them out on my bed. I laid down while Dave took out each staple one at a time. He was extremely skilled and gentle. Thomas stood next to him and watched, so I tried to not scream too loud, just kidding. I honestly didn't scream, but I did cringe a bit because some of the staples were a bit more difficult to remove and it caused me some pain. One staple was extremely difficult to remove the way it was in my skin, so I made sure Dave knew it really hurt. He felt bad and said it was buried in my skin, so he did his best to remove it. In hindsight, I should have taken some pain medication before he removed the staples. I definitely took some when he was done. The scar left behind from the staples was quite large, and you could see exactly where the surgeon opened my abdomen to get to my liver. Recovery was a slow process but slowly I got back to things I enjoyed. Dave, Thomas, and I were involved in the football program by assisting with medical care on the sidelines during the football games. The first home game I was able to attend, I walked extremely slow to get to the field. One of the coaches who knew me looked quite concerned. I don't think he realized I was recovering from a major surgery. I loved the kids, watching the game, and being a part of the team. However, I did not enjoy when a kid was injured. We would have to run out to the field to check on the player and assist him back to the bench. My boys did not play football. I realized how brutal it was on their young bodies. The injuries ranged from concussions, sprains, broken bones, cuts, bruises, and many times, we would send kids to the hospital for serious injuries that needed further medical care. When the boys would score a touchdown, the firefighters would blow the horn on the truck, and everyone would go crazy with excitement. All this support from our community made being a part of this team a great experience. The weather was getting quite cold so a friend of ours brought me a tent with a heater so I could watch one of the games. This is what I love about the people in this community, they're the most generous, kind, and loving people I have ever known. Most people knew Dave because he had a good reputation in our community as a family doctor. They knew his wife had cancer and were extremely supportive of us along the way. When you have such love and support, it was a total game changer for me in how I faced my cancer journey. I faced cancer with people who loved me and my family, so I didn't feel as if I was alone. I had a community who were there to support me and my family during a most difficult time of our lives.

The Year's Ending Celebration

We were now entering the season of Christmas, so this is an extremely busy time for our family. Joseph was coming home from college which brightened my spirits. Thomas and Joshua would be on break too. I loved when the kids were all home, even if they were glued to their Play Station. I loved to see the boys all together and sleeping in their own beds at night. Sometimes they didn't know it, but I would walk in their rooms while they were sleeping, pray over them, and kiss them goodnight. Christmas time was exciting to spend with family, friends, and Dave's office staff. This Christmas was precious to me after enduring my recent surgery. It made me appreciate my family and our traditions even more. We had a family tradition to go to a tree farm with Dave's best friend from high school and his family. After we cut down a beautiful Christmas tree, load it up on the truck, we would have pizza when we got home. Our house was beautifully decorated and so was grandpa's and grandma's house. Not only did Dave put Christmas lights on our house, but he would do his parent's house too. We made time for church service on Christmas Eve. This service was always special because we could spend time praying, singing, listening to God's Word in the sermon and Bible verses, and praise God for sending His son Jesus. Christmas day was spent opening presents and going to Dave's parent's house to open more presents and have a special Lebanese dinner. Dave and I share the Lebanese culture because of our family heritage. I grew up eating the food and sharing many of the traditions, so we had this in common with our relationship. I truly enjoyed the holiday with my family. I still was recovering from surgery but most thankful for every moment. Christmas came to an end, but we still had to prepare for the new year coming, 2017.

2017 A Year of Change

Joseph went back to college, the kids started school again, and I had another PET Scan scheduled. This New Year came so fast, but I could only be thankful to God to see it. I survived longer than was expected with no complications from the treatment or surgery. I was feeling better after just a few months after my surgery. I was sad to see Joseph leave for school, but he had to get back to his baseball team and studies. Thomas was happy to see all his friends at school, and soon he would be playing basketball. Joshua was happy to be playing his trumpet in band class again. It was a lonely time for me having the kids off to school and Dave at work. I spent a lot of my time with Dave's parents. Dave's dad was unable to drive, so I would help where I could. They became my best friends during a difficult time in my life. I would always take them shopping at Meijer, Kroger, or wherever they needed to go. I enjoyed the company, and I was happy to help them out after all they did for me. I eventually went back to the University of Michigan Hospital to have my follow up PET scan. The results were not what we were expecting. The PET scan showed another tumor in the liver and peri-aortic lymph node. We followed up with the oncologist who recommended we see Dr. Cuneo, an Associate Professor in the Radiation Oncology Department who serves as the lead in clinical trials for pancreatic cancer, hepatocellular carcinoma, and colorectal cancer. With these credentials, we felt confident in his opinion for radiation treatment. When we met with him, he was extremely personable. He gave us all the information about radiation therapy and made me feel confident in having radiation treatment to the lymph node. He did not want to radiate the tumor in the liver at this point because he felt it was too small for the radiation to be effective. We scheduled an appointment for later in the month for the treatment to be administered. I needed three days of treatment on Monday, Wednesday, and Friday because he felt it was safer. This treatment is called Stereotactic Body Radiation Therapy (SBRT) which involves a high dose of radiation therapy delivered to a single tumor with use of multiple beam angles that can safely deliver radiation treatment without destroying tissue outside of the tumor marker. I was in tears again, full of anxiety and fear, and extremely disappointed to have to go through more treatment. This treatment was especially traumatic because of the nature of the treatment. The treatment involves laying down on a hard table while a machine passes over the body to deliver radiation beams to fry a specific tumor. I was completely overwhelmed and cried out to the Lord. I did not want to go through this, let alone drive there for three days of treatment. Dave couldn't keep taking time off, so I arranged for some friends to take me for the second and third treatment. Dave went with me to the uptake day or preparation day for treatment. This day was extremely overwhelming and uncomfortable. I had to change into a hospital gown, lay on a hard table with only a pad for support, and stay still as they prepared me for treatment. They did a CT scan and put markings on my body to know exactly where to aim the beam. It was the very first time I had a tattoo. They also had to make a mold of my body so that when I underwent treatment, I would not be able to move while the beams radiated the tumor. I was horrified during this procedure, so I took an Ativan to calm me down. I felt like a laboratory specimen being pushed, poked, turned, and analyzed for viewing under a microscope. Now I understand what it's like for so many women going through breast cancer treatment. This procedure strips your dignity away leaving you to feel helpless and totally dependent on the people in that room to save your life. It was bad enough to go through chemotherapy and two surgeries, but now I had to endure radiation therapy too. It put me in a dark place, and I spent even more time praying, and asking God for help. I wished that God would take it all away and allow me to live freely like so many people without a disease. I was hurt, angry, and frustrated to give so much of myself to endure this procedure along with everything I was already doing as a wife and mother. Then God came to me and calmed the storm that was raging in me. He lifted my spirits and gave me the courage to face this challenge. I honestly knew that I had to do this if I wanted to destroy the cancer. I had to go through this no matter how uncomfortable it was, but I knew God would be with me every step of the way. God helped me to see that I could do far greater things that I thought were possible with Him by my side. I would allow my faith in God to lead the way out of the dark place I was in and allow Him to be the light that leads the way in any storm. God was equipping me to be strong and courageous just like Joshua in the Bible because He knew that I was going to be facing even more hardships when Grandma had a stroke just before I was scheduled for my radiation treatment.

Grandma's Stroke

Sometimes you get the phone call you will regret later. I received a phone call from grandpa one Friday afternoon with panic in his voice. I never even knew if grandpa could remember our phone number let alone successfully dial it at the age of 96. He said that something was wrong with grandma. This startled me not knowing what was going on. My brain was not thinking like a nurse currently with all the personal issues I was going through. My only thought was she fell and broke her hip. We were going to have dinner with them later because she always makes a special Lebanese dinner on Friday's. I was just about to race over there but thought I should call Dave. I called Dave as soon as I got off the phone with grandpa and waited to hear back from him. When he did call me back, I was in utter shock with what he had to say. He told me grandma had a stroke. He called EMS right away and met them at the house. Apparently, she was cooking at the stove and collapsed to the floor so when grandpa saw her, he called us right away. The kids were just getting out of school, so I told Thomas what happened and to meet me at grandma's house with Joshua. I raced over to their house to check on grandpa and found the stove on and the dinner burning. Grandpa was upset so I calmed him down, assisted him in my car with Thomas and Joshua, and drove to the hospital. When we arrived, they already were evaluating her, but they allowed us to come in to see her. She was awake with a right sided facial droop, right sided paralysis, and she could not speak. It was upsetting for all of us to see her in this condition. The doctor told Dave they needed to ship her to a larger hospital in Detroit that had more resources available to treat her stroke. He agreed and they arrange her transport. Dave, Thomas, and grandpa met her at the Emergency Room. I took Joshua home. Dave and Thomas came home just before midnight and brought grandpa to our house to stay the night. We did not want to leave him alone. Dave said the doctors allowed them to sit in the physician's lounge while they waited for grandma to be evaluated and transferred to her room. They started her on a blood thinner to prevent any further clotting to her brain. Normally they would give a patient an IV medication called Tissue Plasminogen Activator (tPA) to help breakdown the clot in her brain, but they felt it was too risky for her to receive this medication. Normally, a patient who is being treated for a stroke must follow the stroke protocol and given this medication within a three-hour time frame. We all got a good night sleep and went to visit her the next morning. I decided to get there early to see what was going on.

Grandma's Stroke

Dave would go later with his dad. For some reason, my brain went into ICU nurse mode, and I couldn't shut it off. It was as if I was back at my job. Honestly, it felt so good to be in nurse mode. I love nursing, it is just in my blood. When I arrived, grandma was in a room with another lady on the medical/surgical unit. She couldn't speak and she couldn't move her right side, so she needed a lot of assistance. The first thing I did was talk to the nurse about what was going on, and if she could be transferred to a private room. They moved her that same day. The nurse said that she would be here in the unit for a few days and then be transferred to the rehabilitation unit down the hall. Days later, she was on the rehabilitation unit learning to function with her limitations. The rehabilitation unit was quite large, the nurses were extremely nice, and she seemed to be adjusting to her routine. Dave's sister came in from Florida and was staying with grandpa in their house to assist him with all his needs. Grandpa could not be left alone for too long for his safety and wellbeing. Grandma didn't stay too long in the hospital rehab unit and was transferred to another rehabilitation facility closer to our home. We were becoming weary of the hour drive back and forth to the hospital in Detroit, so having her closer would be a good decision. The new rehabilitation unit was located directly behind the hospital where Dave saw his patients, so it would be convenient for him to visit his mom after making his rounds. It was not the most pleasant place, but she had a room to herself for a few days. I checked on her daily to make sure she had what she needed. Dave, his sister, and grandpa would visit her in the evening. Grandma's right sided weakness eventually resolved, but she still couldn't speak. Dave's sister returned to Florida and my niece came to stay with grandpa. The family had to make some difficult decisions quickly about care for their parents before grandma was discharged. After many conversations with his family, Dave decided to place his parents in an assisted living home. Nobody wanted to do this, but it was the best choice with the care needs for both his parents. Dave found a place directly across the street from the hospital. We had to move grandpa in first because Dave's niece was not staying much longer. Grandpa was not happy about this move but went along with it because he needed the care. He had people to help him with meals, his medications, bathing, and to check on him often. There were plenty of other residents so he wouldn't be lonely and had many activities to keep him entertained. There were many issues with grandma at the rehab unit to deal with and it took a toll on my mental health. I never realized how many problems would arise from her stroke. It was heartbreaking to watch her endure these trials. While all this was going on, we had to care for our own kids, house, and I was scheduled for three rounds of radiation therapy.

Radiation Therapy

I was not prepared to go through radiation therapy with everything going on with Dave's parents, but I had no choice but to face the procedure. I was grateful that Dave took me to my first treatment. We parked in the visitors parking lot and walked into the building. As we walked, I noticed that the sidewalk was lined with rocks on each side specially painted by patients and families. Each rock had its own message on it that sent chills down my spine. When we arrived at the department, we checked in and sat in a large waiting room. I took an Ativan to calm myself down. As I looked around, my heart just broke to see so many other people suffering with some sort of cancer who needed radiation treatment. I was also extremely grateful that God gifted so many people the opportunity to have this treatment available. When the nurse called me back, I kissed David goodbye, and walked back to a changing room to put a hospital gown on. When I was ready, the nurse took me back to an extremely large room with a large, thick door that shut behind us. I was so afraid, I wanted to cry because I did not want to be there. I felt overwhelmed with fear. I was put on the table, and into the mold they made for me. They kept moving me here and there, placing me precisely where they needed me to be positioned so the radiation beams would hit the correct spot. I was freezing on the table and felt extremely uncomfortable, but they were extremely kind and tried to be gentle while positioning me. Once I was properly positioned, I asked them to cover my eyes with a towel before they left the room. I did not want to see the machines traveling over my face because I'm extremely claustrophobic. When they were finished, they went in a room to watch me through a glass window. They would instruct me over a speaker when I needed to hold my breath as they started the process of the radiation treatment. My heart was racing. I needed to calm down so the Ativan could work, so I said a prayer. During the procedure, I could hear the loud noises of the machines rotating around me. I felt as if I had no control and followed the directions of the technician. After the procedure, they came in the room to help me off the table and told me I was free to go. I was more than happy to leave, change back into my clothes, and see Dave patiently waiting for me in the waiting room. My husband is a saint for what he must endure with caring for all his patients, our family, my cancer issues, his parents' needs, and he never complains. I wish I had his demeanor at times because he looks at everything so logical, where I am an emotional driven person. I can feel someone's pain and sorrow. My strength is being a caretaker and will do everything in my heart to give to others. Both Dave and I are trained to critical think, so I do have skills to assess, evaluate, and plan in the decision-making process. Honestly, we are a great couple because we balance each other out. We approach things differently but come to the same conclusions. Our faith in God is what keeps us grounded and working in the same direction. I've never felt so much love for him in all our years of marriage than our time together facing cancer. My cancer has brought me closer to God, my husband, my family, and all the people in my life. I do my best to show them kindness and generosity, even when I'm struggling with my emotions. Having cancer takes everything you have to fight, leaving you feel empty inside, so it's hard to give of yourself to others. God provides for my needs with His love and grace, so I can love others. My next two treatments were not as traumatic as the first one because I got use to the routine. I had two friends who drove me to these appointments. On the last treatment, they had me ring a bell and presented me with a certificate of completion. This made me feel better because I knew I didn't have to come back. I was proud of myself for facing my fears.

Still More Tragedy

My next step was to follow up with Dr. Cuneo, both oncologists, and have another PET scan in July. They decided to give me a break so my body could heal from everything I went through. Grandma and grandpa were adjusting to the assisted living facility. We felt they were safe there with having their meals cooked for them, medications distributed, help with their daily needs, supervision, and they had other residents to keep them company. Dave and I would sometimes have breakfast with them. I loved all the fancy dishes and sitting at a table with a beautiful tablecloth over it. We would have coffee in fancy cups, so I was having a ball, and the food was good. When Joshua would visit, he would play the grand piano they had in the front lobby for all the residents and their family. He became quite a popular kid there with the residents and they would always be asking when he was coming back to play for them. Thomas loved his grandparents too and would visit with them with his father when he was free. The boys were getting ready to finish school and Joseph was coming home in May. We would visit him in Chicago often during the baseball season. We loved watching him pitch. Coach Ziefert would always ask how I was doing and talk with me when we were there. We didn't get to know the parents like in high school, but they were all friendly to talk to. On his last day of school, we packed him up and brought him home. He played baseball on an adult league when he got home. I couldn't be happier to have Joseph home again sleeping in his own bed in his own room. It just didn't feel right to me for him to be away from home so far away, but he was making responsible decisions, passing all his classes, and enjoying all his new friends.

In the month of May, Dave received a call from the assisted living facility. They informed him that his mother took a fall. Dave rushed to the facility and after examining her, he was sure that she broke her hip. When Dave called me with this news, it broke my heart. I couldn't believe she had fallen and was going to need a hip replacement surgery. Dave took her to see Dr. Wayne who evaluated her and told Dave to take her to get an X-ray. Upon reviewing the X-Ray, they admitted her to the hospital for a hip fracture and put in a consultation for an orthopedic surgeon. Dave's sister flew back from Florida to be with her mom. Dave's brother came but could only stay a few days again. Grandma had a successful surgery and could walk with a walker, but she would need additional therapy in a rehabilitation facility. We did not want to send her to the same rehab, so we went with a new one. This place was cleaner, newer, had nicer rooms, and the care was far better. The staff would come in before her meals, assist her to the bathroom, and help her to the dining area where they would ask her what she would like to eat. When I would visit her, the therapist would tell me about her progress. They were helping her to walk again, and her strength and balance were improving. I was so thankful when she left, that, with tears in my eyes, I gave her therapist a bouquet of white roses. Eventually, she was discharged and went back to the assisted living facility with grandpa. He was so happy to have her back with him. They were a cute couple, him with his wheeling walker and her with her four-prong walker. Dave and I were relieved that they were doing well.

Can We Get a Break?

Despite grandma's fall, rehabilitation, and getting their house ready to be put on the market, we were enjoying the summer. Thomas and Joshua finished school in the middle of June, and we were back to another baseball season with the boys. Joseph was already playing baseball for his team, and Thomas would soon be playing on his dad's team, the Macomb Sting. I enjoyed watching them play, being in the stands with the parents, and going to tournaments out of town. In July, I returned to the hospital to get another PET scan after the radiation therapy. I was saddened to hear that another tumor popped up in the lungs and the liver tumor was growing. So, once again, we followed up with all the doctors. They wanted to observe these tumors because they were too small to treat at the time. They didn't want me to have more chemotherapy because my body needed to get stronger and heal to be able to endure more treatment. The plan was to treat both tumors with radiation therapy which did not thrill me at all, but having more chemotherapy was not exciting either. We would follow up with a PET scan in three months to make a final decision on the best treatment. I was depressed knowing I was going to face further treatment, but I tried to enjoy the summer with the boys. Then, on grandma's birthday, we got a phone call with more tragedy. I was accustomed to the phone waking us up throughout the years with patient or hospital calls for David, but this phone call was different. It was a nurse from the assisted living facility, and I knew something was terribly wrong, but this time it was with grandpa. Dave told the nurse he would be there as fast as he could and hung up the phone. I knew from Dave's voice it was serious, grandpa had collapsed in his room. Grandma called the nurse, who called the ambulance. Dave got dressed and went directly to the hospital, while I went to check on grandma. When I saw she was with the nurse, I also rushed to the hospital Emergency Room. I knew grandpa was in bad shape the moment I saw him. A respiratory therapist was assisting him to breath with a resuscitation breathing bag. This bag forces oxygen into the lungs. Looking at the heart monitor, and seeing the looks on the nursing staff, my friends, were all in tears. The most shocking thing was that the doctor wanted to transfer him to the ICU and place him on a ventilator. I was extremely angry at this point because I knew that these were not grandpa's wishes. Dave was extremely upset and was talking with his siblings on the phone. I suggested we stop bagging him and let him pass. The nurses looked at me with approval, but the doctor said he needed to talk to Dave. The final decision was to let grandpa go. By that time, our pastor, our deacon, and the boys were all there. We said a prayer and our final goodbyes, and as soon as the respiratory therapist stopped bagging him, grandpa died. Grandpa was 96 years old, lived a good life, and knew he wanted to be with the Lord. Grandpa made it clear to us that when it was his time to die, that he did not want his life to be prolonged, so we followed his wishes. Tears flowed from my eyes. This was the hardest thing to face after going through all the other health crises. The pastor and the deacon took the boys to Subway for lunch, and I was extremely thankful. Dave and I went to tell grandma who was quite devastated. The nursing staff was also heart broken. The nursing staff and everyone at the facility loved grandpa because he was so friendly, told them so many stories, and was the kindest soul. Dave decided to spend the night with his mom, until his sister and brother arrived the next day to prepare for the funeral. The service was done at our church, Immanuel Lutheran Church, where grandma and grandpa were members. It was a beautiful service and I arranged for a luncheon to be served in the Family Life Center. After the luncheon, some men from the military came and did a 21-gun salute because grandpa served in WWII. When they were done with the ceremony, they folded the American flag, and presented it to grandma. This was a very emotional and memorable experience. We respect and hold dear all the men and women who serve our country. The immediate family members proceeded to the cemetery where they had a special ceremony before they put grandpa in his gravesite. We all went home filled with so many emotions, but it felt good to see everyone together again. This was going to be a difficult time for our family because grandpa was such a great man. He was a man of great faith, loved his family, and loved others with his cheerful spirit and kind heart. He was highly intelligent even with only a high school graduate level education. He worked as a tool maker his whole life as he provided for his family. He wanted his kids to go to college and have a good life. We all loved grandpa and would miss him dearly. Grandma would have to get accustomed to being alone after 62 years of marriage. My boys loved their grandpa. He taught them about God, history, and many life lessons. He was always there at all their school activities. He was an honorable man, someone my boys looked up to, and would be greatly missed. We were comforted that grandpa will live with God for eternity, and that one day we will all be with him again.

More Radiation Therapy

Through the many trials we faced, our faith is what brings us through them. I was struggling when we took Joseph back to college in Chicago. I didn't want to leave him alone with everything going on with our family. I knew he would continue to do well in school, baseball, and make good decisions. He had a great support system with the baseball team. Maybe my worrying was a way of distracting myself from focusing on my own issues. Except, when you worry, you take away the power of God. I knew God would take care of everything throughout our lives. I was becoming a regular in the PET scan department and I knew exactly what to expect when I got there. I would drink the Barium and would joke with the staff about wanting it to be a Sangria instead. The results were once again not what we wanted to hear. There was a mild progression to the liver and lung lesions. Now it was time for more radiation treatment, but this time it would be to the liver. The doctor said the lung tumor was too small to treat with radiation so we would watch it closely. The treatment to the liver was going to consist of three rounds of radiation and would require me to use a simulation mask. I had a special day set up to watch a video and train me how this procedure would work. The simulation mask was used to observe my respirations by watching a screen that showed waves when I took a breath. When I held my breath, I would see a flat line. In addition to the mask, they inserted a large tube in my mouth to bite down on to simulate my breathing. I would be taking deep breaths, breathe normal, and hold my breath while watching the screen in the mask. This breathing technique assisted the doctors in administering radiation treatment. While breathing, your liver moves up and down. I had to hold my breath so my liver wouldn't move. This helped them aim the beam directly at the tumor. The advanced technology they were using was extremely impressive, so I was thanking God again for another lifesaving procedure. I was not as upset during this procedure as I was with my first radiation treatment. I had adjusted to the routine, so I felt more at ease. This procedure was somewhat difficult and time consuming while doing many trials of simulation. Again, Dave took me to my preparation appointment, my first treatment, and my friends drove me to the final two. After my treatment was complete, I rang the bell, and they gave me another certificate of completion. I don't think I would have been able to get through this procedure if the staff was not so amazing. They were so kind and patient when I was there, so I was immensely thankful. We followed up

More Radiation Therapy

with the doctor who scheduled me for my next PET scan in January 2018. The treatment had no major side effects but would leave me feeling fatigued. The only thing that kept me positive was a trip to Florida to spend time with Joseph while he played baseball.

2018 Florida Trip

The next PET scan in January showed further progression in the right lung and a new retroperitoneal lymph node site. This was devastating to me. I had already been through two radiation treatments, and I knew that this meant I would be facing more chemotherapy. I was extremely discouraged. I wanted to see an end to this disease and get to remission. I also was afraid of dying or something going wrong. Every time I found out I had a new tumor, it felt like a death sentence. If my PET scans were clear, then I would have felt more confident in my prognosis. I would have had more time to recover from each treatment. The oncologist decided to treat me with an oral chemotherapy agent, Xeloda. I would take this twice a day for two weeks then off for one week. He felt that this would make it much easier for our vacation and I wouldn't have to travel to the clinic for chemotherapy. I started this extremely expensive medication just before we left on vacation, and it had terrible side effects. Spring break for Joshua did not fall on the same week as Joseph's, so we had to pull him out of school a week early. Unfortunately, Thomas could not go with us because he was leaving for his senior cruise and did not want to miss school and baseball practice. I booked a four-bedroom condominium in a private condo-association. It looked like something on HGTV. This was Joshua's first time having his own room, bathroom, and queen size bed on vacation. Our place was within walking distance to the private pool, lazy river, gym, and food center that was enclosed by a locked fence. Dave and I loved exercising in the gym area in the early morning and lounging around the pool while Joshua enjoyed swimming and floating on a tube in the lazy river. We were able to see Joseph at the baseball complex. This was exciting because we hadn't seen him since he went back to school. I stayed with Joshua at the condominium some days because he wanted to hang out by the pool and left Dave watch Joseph play. After the game, we were able to have dinner with him and then drive him back to his team's house for the evening. I was on the last few pills of the Xeloda when we arrived, so I had a few days I didn't feel well. I had the chills and felt quite nauseated which put a damper on my vacation. Joseph had one day off from baseball to spend with his family, so we went to the local aquarium, dinner, and back to our condo. Joseph stayed with us that night in his own room. After breakfast Dave took him back to the team. Our vacation was filled with so many good memories, it was difficult to leave, and say goodbye to Joe. When we arrived home, I became quite ill from the oral chemotherapy after taking it for only a few weeks. I was in tears discussing my symptoms: horrible stomach pains, fatigue, and my palms were turning blue. I was told to immediately stop taking the medication and we would follow up with a PET scan in April. I was extremely happy to be off the medication because it made me feel so ill. I was thankful we had such a wonderful vacation which helped me cope with the issues I had to deal with after taking the chemotherapy. Despite having cancer, I thanked God for allowing me to be able to watch my son play baseball in Florida, stay at a beautiful condominium, and enjoy my time with my family.

Graduation 2018

I was getting ready for Thomas to graduate from high school, so I had to plan another graduation party. Thomas had a lot of friends, and we were friends with all their parents, so this would be a big party. I had to plan the meal, send out the invitations, make the picture posters, and get the house ready. Before his graduation, I had yet another PET scan. The scan showed the tumors responding well to treatment, but I still needed to continue with chemotherapy. The doctor decided to put me back on my previous regime of Avastin and 5FU for eight weeks and repeat the PET scan upon completion. I was not looking forward to going back on this treatment again, but the doctor explained that some people cannot tolerate the oral form of chemotherapy. I had to make sure my treatments didn't fall on the week of Thomas's commencement or his graduation party. In addition to Thomas's party, we had many more parties we were invited to. Going back to the clinic was an emotional experience but my nurse Patty welcomed me back with a beautiful smile. She listened to me cry as she administered the treatment. After treatment every other Tuesday, I would go home again with the 5FU pump and return to the clinic on Thursday for them to discontinue it. I would usually experience the same side effects of nausea, fatigue, and felt ache. After a few days I would feel better for the next week and start treatment again the following Tuesday. This was going to be my routine until my next PET scan in July, praying the chemotherapy would completely shrink the tumors. I continued my chemotherapy treatments while we prepared Thomas for graduation and as he got ready for college. There is so much to do with preparing your child for college. Thomas wanted to become a physician and followed his father's footsteps by attending Wayne State University. I was relieved because I felt comfort in knowing if there was any emergency, we could get to him quickly. This decision gave me time to focus on my treatments and his graduation. The morning of his graduation was awards day where I would again give out the Hindy Strong Scholarship. I always gave a short inspirational speech before I presented the award to a few deserving students. Thomas was awarded a few scholarships himself being such an honorable student. He was in the top ten of his graduating class and was well liked by his teachers and peers. Thomas was the kid who showed others determination, perseverance, and passion to succeed. I was extremely proud of him as his mom and was excited to see some of his friends' names called for different scholarships too. In the evening we attended the graduation on the football field.

Graduation 2018

Watching my second son graduate was a special day for me. I thanked God for allowing me to be here for this moment when my life didn't look too promising when I first was diagnosed. Even though I went through many trials and troubles, it was all worth it being able to see my son graduate at this moment. Thomas is so special to me, and I love him with all my heart. His graduation party turned out to be a success. Moreover, we moved Joseph into an apartment in Chicago close to his college. I still was enduring chemotherapy treatment, but God gave me the strength to endure all what we did this summer. I was praising God that I was able to see my boys graduate from high school and be a part of their lives.

Ongoing Treatment

I had another PET scan July 2018 that showed slight improvement. I still had a pulmonary nodule in my right middle lobe of my lung and the lymph node in my periaortic area. I continued my chemotherapy treatment every other week in hopes of shrinking all tumors in my body. My next PET scan was scheduled for October. There was a new routine in my life between chemotherapy, scans, blood work, and visits to the doctors. I was thankful for Dave being able to take time off work for all my scans and doctor visits. I was able to drive myself to my chemotherapy visits because the clinic was only 20 minutes away and I was generally healthy. I had to coordinate everything else around my treatments. The best part of this summer was enjoying my boys being home. The baseball season was going strong, and we continued to live life despite any issues. Grandma was doing quite well, was able to walk around with no issues after her hip surgery and was still a part of our family. Every Sunday, we would pick her up for church and bring her back to our house for dinner. She tried her best to help us with as much as she could.

We would take her grocery shopping when she needed items at her apartment and helped her in any way she needed. Thankfully all the staff at the assisted living center were especially kind to her. She loved spending time with them at the front desk. She still could not talk, but they seemed to understand her anyway. We did our best to keep our family on course with all our activities during that summer. I loved the warmer weather because I could get outside and enjoy the fresh air. I also enjoyed planting my flowers around the house. I plant a considerable number of flowers that wrap from the driveway to the side of the house. They look so beautiful once they start growing and I get so many compliments that it makes me feel special. I believe that when you go through an illness that you must find joy in the little things. I enjoyed the fresh air, beautiful sunshine, and watching my flowers grow. I also enjoy mowing the lawn in the summer too. I love the sounds of the birds while I'm slowly pushing the mower across the lawn. I get a good suntan while I'm doing this, and it gives me time to reflect on life. After I'm done with the lawn, I enjoy looking at how nice it all looks with my flowers blooming. Our landscaping is beautiful, and we keep all the bushes trimmed too.

Having things to enjoy and look forward to helps you from developing depression during an illness. I am thankful that my health allows me to do so much in my life. I realize that many people who have cancer are not so fortunate, but I still believe that finding something you enjoy is important. Many days when I am not feeling well, resting on the couch, and watching television is all I can do. This is when I try to find a program that entertains me and keeps my mind off my illness. There are other times where rest is all I can do to get through the side effects of the treatment. There is no shame in napping, relaxing, or lounging around when you're not physically capable of much else, but it's important to stay as active as you can. Sometimes I would do an activity and find myself fatigued afterwards, so I would sit on my chair to rest and spend time on the computer. I love the game of Spider Solitaire so I would play a game until I won. I enjoy this game because it challenges my mind to think, and it's like a puzzle to me. Playing this game also helps me to get my mind off the nausea or feeling ache, especially when I won. Some people will enjoy reading books when they're ill, but I am not one to read. I have always had trouble reading books. My mind wanders, and my eyes get tired if I read for too long. I prefer playing cards more than reading a book. I believe it's important to find things you enjoy and spend time with those you love.

Feelings after Treatment

Cancer treatment can be brutal and comes with so many emotions. I would become impatient, frustrated, and look to God for some relief. Many people are going through far worse than me, so I try not to feel too sorry for myself or get too down. I always praise God for all my blessings and try to keep an upbeat approach. I don't know how to express myself somedays with all that I have endured and must go through in the future. I see more blood tests, scans, doctors' visits, and treatments, but I don't see an end. Dave and everyone in my life did their best to keep my spirits up so I didn't get too down or discouraged. Despite all this support, there were days where nothing is fine. Dave understands how hard these days are for me, and for our whole family. He did everything he could to help me feel better. He was a pillar of strength for me, but I didn't know how to tell him how I feel. I was hurting inside and felt lost and in a lonely place. I felt like I was on an island waiting for a ship to come and save me. Isolation, fear, frustration, discouraged, but you push yourself beyond measures just to get through each day. God is that ship.

He sends constant reminders that He's still there with me so I can get through each treatment. He sends great people who show me unconditional love and support. I am passionate about people. I try to use my illness to show people that no matter how bad things are, God is there and provides the strength to persevere. I believe it's vitally important to be honest and allow people to hear your story, to discuss your issues, and to be as real as possible. I believe that if you hold it all in and don't talk about your feelings, it could set you further into the darkness. Sometimes this may mean it's best to seek professional help. I have a Christian counseling center that I visit once a month. This helps me to discuss my issues with a professional who gives me ways to cope with my disease. I don't feel any shame talking about this because I know I'm doing what is best for me to heal both physically and emotionally. I believe that a person must heal from within and that includes mind, body, and spirit.

2019 Still more Chemotherapy

I was looking forward to a new year without chemotherapy, but I just couldn't catch a break. We had an amazing Christmas and New Year with the boys being home from college. Again, they were back at school plugging away with their studies. Joshua was also excelling. He adjusted to his brothers being gone. What more could I ask for during my treatment then to see my boys all doing well. My next PET scan was done in January, but I was not happy with the results. The lung nodule didn't change, but the peri-aortic lymph node increased in size and metabolic activity. This meant one thing, I would continue chemotherapy because the site was radiated before. It was too dangerous according to Dr. Cuneo to radiate that area without damaging other organs in the area. He felt it was safer for me to continue chemotherapy. With tears in my eyes, I acknowledged his decision and went back for continued chemotherapy treatment despite the side effects. I continued chemotherapy until April. This put me on tract for a year of chemotherapy. My body was taking abuse from the drugs with weight gain, fatigue, and gastritis. My mouth tasted like metal so everything I ate had a bitter taste, so I did not enjoy food. After dinner, I would often put a piece of candy in my mouth just so I could taste something good. This was not a good habit to fall into, but it helped me with my taste buds and lack of appetite. I had to endure this because my goal was to get to remission. You must focus on a goal to overcome the challenges of chemotherapy treatment. Sometimes it's as simple as showering after having the pumped removed. For me, my goals were simple, I wanted to spend time with my family. They kept me going strong.

A Well Needed Break

It was a long, hard year of chemotherapy. I was quite exhausted from the treatments. The PET scan in March, was relatively stable with no new growths and lung nodule unchanged. The oncologist recommended a two-month break from treatment, and another scan at the end of that time. This news was refreshing to hear. The year of chemotherapy took so much away from my life and family. My body was plagued by fatigue, weight gain, and anxiety. Having this time off would give me time to heal. I needed to heal both physically and emotionally. A year is a long time when you're taking every other week out of your life to sit in a clinic receiving chemotherapy. It's a year of nausea, fatigue, body aches, headaches, and feeling awful for three to five days post treatment. Now my goal was to get back to exercising, watching my diet, and trying to get a few pounds off. As I got older, my metabolism slowed down, I was not as active as I wanted to be, and I found comfort in eating too much. This resulted in gaining a few pounds. I decided to work with a personal trainer to give me new exercises I could do at the gym. Most of my exercises consisted of cardio, and weight training. My trainer explained to me that you burn more fat with weights as you build more muscle. I would work with her twice a week and the other days do other exercises she taught me along with cardio. I had to be realistic and not expect drastic changes because I was not that overweight. My goal was to tone my body, get stronger in case I needed further treatment, and stabilize my emotions. I always felt so much better after a hard workout at the gym. Working out made me feel a sense of accomplishment. I would take a shower when I got home which made me feel like a whole new person. This routine was continued over the break I had from treatment, but I also wanted to do something to use my nursing skills. I signed up to volunteer at Troy Beaumont Hospital. Volunteering has changed over the years, and I was treated like a paid employee. I had to have an interview, take on-line classes for safety and regulations, and attend a three-hour orientation. After this I was placed in the Intensive Care Unit to help the staff. I was extremely excited to be in my favorite place in the hospital. However, I didn't feel like I belonged there with the way the staff treated me. I was greeted by a patient care technician who directed me to stock the shelves. This was a very tedious job, but I knew it was important for the staff to have supplies necessary for patient care. I was quite familiar with the supplies I had to stock in the closets but wasn't given many directions. I tried to be friendly with the staff, but they didn't seem too interested in having conversations with me. What they didn't know was I once did their job and was a master's prepared nurse educator. I would watch them take care of the patients from the window and it almost brought me to tears because I missed working so much. I watched one nurse who seemed quite skilled at taking care of her patient on the ventilator. All I thought of was the days I worked in the ICU when I was a nurse. I loved taking care of my patients, but I was best at educating the patient and family about what I was doing, the disease process, and goals for the future. I wanted to do something more significant than stocking shelves, so I asked to be transferred to the Emergency Department. They needed help in this area, but I would have to be trained on the job duties. It was a busy place with patients lined up in the hallways for hours. I was still recovering from my yearlong treatment, so I paced myself when doing rounds. What was great about this position was I had the opportunity to work with other volunteers who were in college. I loved working with them because they were extremely friendly, and we would talk a lot about working in the hospital. We had some good times working together washing down the carts after patients left and putting new linen on them for new patients. We would also help with cleaning the rooms for the new patients. The place was busy with patients being wheeled from one place to another. We were busy wheeling patients to be discharged, bringing carts back and forth to different areas, cleaning carts, and doing rounds. We also checked on all the patients and ask them if they needed anything. I loved working in the Emergency Room because I saw things that I was not privy to during my years working in a small community hospital. I had an alarming experience with security, police, and many nurses trying to deal with a combative patient. I hate to see patients become violent after they drank too much and were coming down from their high. I discovered all kinds of people who came from different cultures, religions, races, and beliefs. The hospital had a system in place to keep patients moving as quickly as possible so they wouldn't be laying on a cart all day waiting for a bed. The only problem is trying to find a bed in the hospital that was opened to transfer them to. I was quite tired after being on my feet for four hours and the hour drive to and from. I did this once a week and made it home so I could pick Joshua up from high school. With Thomas and Joseph being away at college, I had to drive Joshua to and from school. He was a busy kid with a lot of activities after school. He was busy with band, quiz bowl, bowling, and helping at our church with the audio/visuals, and occasionally playing in the church band. I was able to do activities myself during the day before he came home from school. I would also attend Bible class with some lady friends at our church once a week. They were instrumental in uplifting me with support, prayers, cards, and kindness. I tried to stay active and enjoy my two-month break before my next PET scan. God shines the light through my activities, family, and friends.

PET Scan June 2019

*I*n June of 2019, I had another PET scan that showed more progression of the disease. Both the liver and lung tumor seemed to progress in size, so we decided to go with radiation therapy to get rid of both. Radiation therapy was difficult to endure again for the third time for the liver and then in a few months I would have it to my lung. I didn't know what to think any more, but I continued to rely on my faith. I knew God would give me the strength to get through this despite how I felt inside. I didn't have time to fall apart with three children and my husband. I didn't want my cancer to distract them from what they needed to do in their lives. I tried to protect them from the pain I was going through and made them feel confident that I could handle it. It takes time to arrange radiation therapy after a PET Scan. First, I had to discuss the PET Scan with Dr. Krauss, set up another appointment with Dr. Cuneo, set up simulation, and then I would get three additional radiation treatments. This took time to arrange in addition to the travel time back and forth to the hospital. This takes a lot of patience to deal with, but the hospital was amazing in setting up all the appointments in a timely manner. Life doesn't stop while you go through all these procedures, tests, appointments so I would just take it day by day. You cry, you get down, you're frustrated, depressed, and feel so many emotions that it is hard to process everything going on. Our family relied on our faith to get us through this, and we did everything to support one another. The procedure for radiating the liver and lung was not easy. They had to simulate my breathing while they radiated the specific tumor in the liver. This was no easy procedure for me to do, but I was familiar with the routine from the last treatment. I was finished within an hour and had to come back two more times for a complete dose of radiation. I was relieved to have this procedure completed, but I had to repeat it in my lung area in October. In December, I was scheduled for another colonoscopy which was clear, so I was able to enjoy the Christmas holiday with the boys being home from college.

COVID-19 Hits

COVID-19 Coronavirus disease started appearing in the United States by the late months of 2019. This is an infectious disease caused by the coronavirus, SARS-COV-2 which is a contagious respiratory illness that came from China and affected the world. This virus was spreading quite rapidly, and thousands were dying from it. The government shut down each state and only allowed essential businesses to remain open. Every state followed their own guidelines, but Michigan had some of the strictest rules to follow. Eventually, everyone was required to wear a mask when going into any business to prevent the spreading of this respiratory virus. Dave was going into work, but he saw only acute patients. They had to change many policies of practice that required social distancing, wearing masks, protective gear, and limiting patient contact. He would see some patients virtually over the computer. Many doctors could not do surgeries unless it was an emergency. Hospitals were overwhelmed with the number of patients coming through the doors and the equipment they needed was scarce. The hospital staff were overwhelmed with the admissions, extremely sick people, and many were dying. This virus turned into a political battle, media frenzy, differences of opinions, anger, division, and fear mongering. Our state and country were suffering spiritually because we were trying to look for answers in man without turning to God first. I thought this would bring us together, more people would grow closer to God, and people would be helping each other, but this did not happen. People were vile, full of anger, and fear. This was preventing people from living their lives and many suffered dire consequences as a result. I turned to God and ask Him for guidance in this. God calmed my heart and soul during this difficult time. His love is constant even in the dark days and shines the light of hope. Evil exists in this world and bad things happen, but turning to God is what guides us, strengthens us, and calms our fears. We need to have faith and not fear, trust that God has a plan, and trust Him to lead the way. People were dealing with this by turning to government officials and not God. I prayed every day and asked God for guidance. I was feeling quite depressed to see our nation suffer through this. People were angry, depressed, and were hopeless. It didn't help when our governor locked down everything for such a long time. People were even afraid to go to the emergency room for fear they would contract this disease. Many people couldn't get their health care needs met because doctors were limited in their practices. What made me angry was the abortion clinics were considered essential. Many people couldn't get their hip replacement done, others couldn't get their health care treatments, and so many couldn't get in to see the doctor. We thought this would only last until the hospitals were not so overwhelmed. When the curve started going down, hospitals were in better shape, treatments to combat this virus became available, our state still would not open anything. This became problematic because thousands of people were out of work and unable to pay their bills, businesses were closing, schools were experiencing issues with technology and virtual learning. Everyone was getting tired of being regulated by a tyrannical governor who used this for her political agenda. While other states were opening and experiencing good outcomes, we were forced beyond reasonable measures to limit our ability to leave our homes. Thankfully, my oncologist's office was still open for my cancer treatment, but not everyone was able to get diagnostic and follow-up tests for theirs. This saddened me because I know how important it is to find answers before tumors grow or a disease ends up in the latent stages of treatment. Everyone was full of fear, anger, and wanted answers. It was difficult to listen to the bantering back and forth without having a medical understanding of what they were talking about. Many people started to shame, bash, and say nasty things, so I stayed out of those conversations and tried to give a positive voice of reason. Honestly, I totally understand how everyone felt. This virus took us by surprise, and no one was immune from the life-threatening affects it had. Everyone had to follow the guidelines set out by each state governor until hospital admissions were under control. They even shut down the churches, so we watched church on-line from home. It's not the same watching church from home. You miss out on so much fellowship, music, and worshiping in God's House. The gym was closed so I tried to exercise to different workouts I downloaded to the television. Life changed, people changed, and it was impossible to drive without noticing how empty the streets were. Everything was closed except for the grocery stores and bigger chain stores for home equipment. I still had to get my blood work and treatment done every other week, so I was thankful they didn't close the oncology clinic. By fall, things started to open, and people were going back to work but our state still had the most stringent lockdown rules.

We cancelled our vacation we had planned in March, but we all were able to go to Hilton Head, South Carolina in July. The southern states were open for the most part, so this was going to be a family vacation I was going to enjoy. Joseph came home during the pandemic and completed his last semester of college on-line. We convinced Thomas to go with us even though he still was in school. Everything was online so he brought his computer and would work on his homework when he could. We had a beautiful condo that faced the beach with two twin beds and bathroom for Joe and Joshua, a king size bed and bathroom for Dave and me, and Thomas slept in the living room on a queen size sofa sleeper. We had a huge balcony with a large table and chairs for us to have breakfast in the morning while watching the ocean waves, people, and sun rise. We also had a huge kitchen, living room table, and washer and dryer which came in handy. The beach was amazing, the sun was hot, and the ocean was cool. We had plenty of things to do from sightseeing, golfing, touring a naval and battleship, a boat ride to a fort, miniature golf, and enjoying the beach. It was a great get away with everything that was going on in Michigan. We were able to go out to eat and most places were open if you wore a mask. This was an incredibly special vacation to spend with my family because Thomas eventually went back to his apartment and Joe found a job working in Portage, Michigan. I was extremely excited for him that he would be working only three hours away and would be living close to my best friend, Linda, and her husband. My heart sank saying goodbye to him, but I was extremely proud of him working full-time making a decent salary for his age. 2020 was a rough year with so many ups and downs, but my family was healthy, doing well, and God leads us every step of the way.

COVID Diagnosis March 2021

*A*s much as I tried to avoid catching COVID for a whole year, I became infected in March, and it hit me hard. I have no idea where or when I picked this virus up. I wore my mask, social distanced, washed my hands, kept away from sick people but unfortunately, it didn't spare me a visit to the hospital. I received my treatment as usual the first week of March, but something was different this time. I experienced a migraine headache so bad that nothing would take away the pain. I ended up with nausea and vomiting all night until it finally settled down. I have had this reaction before, but this time it seemed to hit me harder. All week I just didn't feel myself and I told Dave I just wasn't feeling too great. He attributed it all to chemotherapy so I continued life as normal and rested when I could. By Monday, I felt well enough to go with him to the gym and I did a 30-minute rowing machine workout. Dave likes it when I come to the gym with him, and I felt as if I needed to get back into my exercise routine. Exercising helps me feel so much better after my treatment both emotionally and physically. I normally go every day after my treatment, but by Tuesday I felt tired, chills, and not myself so I just rested on the couch all day. I attributed my symptoms to my chemotherapy treatment. By Wednesday, I was feeling better and went back to the gym to do another workout, but when I went to the gym on Thursday, I just didn't feel the same. That evening I went with Dave to Joshua's quiz-bowl tournament. I told him that I wasn't feeling too good, felt fatigued, chills, and not my usual self. The tournament was awesome, and Joshua's team came in third place. When we got home, the chills started to get worse, so I got some blankets and stayed on the couch. The next day, I didn't feel any better, in fact, I felt even worse. I had no appetite, felt extremely fatigued, and just slept all day. Dave was concerned and wanted me to eat and drink, but I had no desire for food, and nothing tasted good. We were planning to visit Joe Saturday to get his luggage before our trip to Florida, so I was looking forward to this visit more than anything. Sadly, when it came down to leaving that Saturday morning, Dave had to go without me. He thought it would be good for me to go for a ride and get out of the house, but I felt as if a truck hit me, and I decided to just rest. He was concerned leaving me alone, but Joshua was home to help me. He decided to go for the day and got back by evening. This was a most difficult day for me as I was getting weaker, I had diarrhea, couldn't eat or drink much of anything, and felt awful. I kept calling Dave and telling him what I was going through. He reassured me everything was going to be fine and make sure to eat and drink. I told him that I almost passed out bringing ramen noodle soup to Joshua. I was extremely weak, and I felt my breathing was compromised. Dave came home that evening and watched me closely. We decided not to go to church the next day, but just pray at home. He wanted to keep a close eye on me because I was getting worse. What worried me the most was I had another treatment scheduled that Tuesday, and I didn't know how I was going to get through it feeling so ill. I called the clinic on Monday and the nurse told me to go to the hospital to get a COVID test done. After the test was complete, I called my doctor because I felt I was getting weaker and shorter of breath. He called me in an antibiotic and told me to take Vitamin C, Zinc, and Vitamin D. Tuesday morning, my portal from University of Michigan Hospital messaged me that I was COVID positive. It hit me like a ton of bricks. I didn't know what to think. All I knew was I wanted to get better soon because we had a vacation planned for Florida in two weeks. Joshua was bringing his friend Trevor, and Joseph was flying out there on Saturday, so we had to pick him up at the airport on our way down. By Wednesday, Dave was genuinely concerned about me, especially when I called him at work and told him that my breathing was getting worse. He came home right away, gave me a breathing treatment, checked my oxygen saturation, listened to my lungs, and decided that we should go to the hospital to get a chest X-Ray.

When we got to the Emergency Room, I was struggling with my breathing, so they got me into a bed right away. They told me that I was going to be admitted for COVID. They would follow the protocol of antivirals, steroids, a blood thinner, vitamins, and convalescent plasma. The Emergency Room staff were awesome and soon I was wheeled to my new room in the ICU. After 15 years working in the ICU, I was going to be a patient there. It felt scary getting in a bed where I took care of people in the same room. It was nice to see familiar faces of my peers and physicians that I worked with. God sent me angels to care for me. They got me in bed, hooked up the monitor, oxygen, IV fluids, and soon the infectious disease doctor came in to see me. Everyone who came in the room was gowned up with special protective gear, face masks, gowns, gloves, so they would not contaminate anyone else they cared for that day. I was in isolation, and it didn't hit me how sick I was until I had to get up to go to the bathroom. It was a chore because I had to drag my IV pump, oxygen tubing, and heart monitor that was too short to reach the toilet. I had to disconnect them until I was done. I was discouraged, so they allowed Dave to visit me, but he had to wear all the protective gear too. He was such a trooper because he had to sterilize everything at home, so Joshua didn't get sick. He washed all the blankets I had on me, disinfected everything in the house, and washed all the clothes. He still had to go to work but would visit me after hours and early in the morning. I was very saddened to be so sick in the hospital, but the nurses were so kind to me, and they cheered me up. My potassium level was quite low from not eating and drinking in addition to having diarrhea, so the nurse gave me oral and IV potassium. The potassium pill was large, so she was kind enough to crush it and put it in apple sauce. The IV potassium started to burn in my arm. The nurse slowed down the drip, so I wasn't in so much pain. I worked with Wendy for years and I was so thankful she was my nurse. I tried to sleep at night, but it was difficult because I was woken up for vitals, blood work done, and a chest x-ray every morning. I decided it was a good idea to sit in a chair to expand my lungs. Then the infectious disease doctor, the pulmonologist, and the primary care doctor would all listen to my lungs and check on how I was doing. I had pneumonia in both my lungs, so they were a bit concerned. The most difficult part of my admission was I had no appetite and the food was awful. I barely ate anything while I was there because everything tasted so nasty. The only thing that I enjoyed was the coffee, but I would only take a few sips. I tried to watch television, but nothing seemed to help me with the boredom and anxiety I was feeling. I was upset because I couldn't watch the Christian TBN station with all my favorite pastors on it because they only had the Catholic station. I prayed every day and asked God to help me recover, but I felt so lonely and in the dark. I didn't want to talk to anyone despite people calling me, I couldn't focus on anything, and all

I wanted to do was sleep. I could barely keep my eyes open when Dave would visit me, because I was not feeling well at all. I was running a fever at times, getting chills, and felt extremely weak. Every day the nurses would give me my medications and helped me with anything I needed. I really wanted a shower, but I could only do a basic sponge bath by the sink and change my gown if I had the energy. After a few days I asked the doctor if I needed the IV to keep running continuously at such a high rate? He told the nurse to stop the additional fluids. I still felt like a nurse and could critical think. The infectious disease doctor said I was getting too many fluids and ordered me some Lasix to get rid of it. Lasix is a diuretic, it makes you pea, so I was up all night in the bathroom which made me miserable. The next morning, I was exhausted, but my lungs sounded less congested according to the doctor. I was getting better each day, but one day Dave brought Joshua in the ICU just to see me from outside the door which cheered me up. I couldn't have any visitors while I was in the hospital, but it was special to have Dave come in as one of the doctors to check on me. I was in the hospital for one week and they said I was able to go home. I lost almost 10 pounds and I needed oxygen when I got home. Dave brought me clothes from home which were quite big on me, but I felt better getting dressed. Despite going home, I was still weak and barely could walk far without getting short of breath. I was extremely worried because we were leaving for

Florida on Friday. I was still extremely fatigued, weak, and not feeling good. Dave felt that it was better for me to go and recover in the sun then to sit home in the cold weather on the couch. I didn't want to disappoint everyone so I agreed to go knowing it would be a difficult journey. I didn't do much of anything for a few days while I was home. Joshua was doing online classes due to COVID precautions at the school, so I felt safe if anything happened to me. I loved when Joshua would put on episodes of House, a series about a brilliant doctor who solves medical challenges with his team of doctors. It's a dramatic show, far from reality, but we both enjoyed watching it, and it passed the time. I still didn't have much of an appetite, it was hard to eat much of the chicken Dave made for dinner. The hospital dropped off oxygen tanks, tubing, and a portable tank, but I barely used oxygen. I was strong enough to get around, complete chores, and pack for vacation.

Spring Break Vacation

I couldn't believe that three days after being discharged from the hospital we were going on a vacation. Joshua's friend Trevor was coming with us on our vacation to St. Augustine, Florida, and we were picking Joe up from the airport on Saturday on our way to the condominium. We had to leave by 4 a.m. so we did not hit the traffic going into Detroit. We were all packed in the car, said a prayer, and Dave led the way to our first stop in Ohio at a Tim Horton's for doughnuts and a bathroom break. I didn't get out of the car because it was chilly outside, and I was comfortable with my blanket. I got out of the car when we stopped at Panera Bread and ordered a breakfast sandwich which was very good. It was a long drive to our hotel room in North Carolina, before we departed the next morning for our second half of the trip to Florida. It was nice to take a warm shower and sleep in a comfortable bed, but I started having abdominal pain and cramping. I ended up not getting much sleep, but we were on the road early to pick Joe up at the airport and start our vacation. We arrived at the airport just in time to have Joe's flight to land and he was able to meet us outside in front of the building. I was so happy to see him, especially after my hospital experience. It was difficult to be in the hospital for a week, so spending time with my family was a Blessing from God. We eventually arrived at the condo, which was smaller than I thought it would be, but it was clean, had two separate bedrooms, two bathrooms, a kitchen, living room, washer, dryer, and a balcony to sit on to look at the ocean from the side of the building. The condo was within walking distance to the beach. We unpacked everything, went out to dinner, and went to a local grocery store. I wasn't up for too much other than lounging on the beach. We found beach chairs in the closet, which was nicer than sitting on a beach towel on the sand. The weather was beautiful, especially in the morning, so we would sit on the balcony to have our coffee each morning and watch the ocean view. Every day the boys would find things to do like golfing, walking around town, going to the lighthouse, and one day I went with them to a fort downtown. The funniest story of our trip is when Trevor ordered a school bus for dinner. It was two grilled cheese sandwiches with a hamburger in between. We couldn't believe how large it was and he ate the whole thing. Most days, I let them do what they wanted to do while I rested in the condo. We would go to the beach every day, but the water was too cold and rough to go swimming. I was still healing and having trouble with abdominal pain. Dave had to call in a prescription to help me, because the pain was getting so bad at night. One day after dinner, we walked along the boardwalk to look at the ocean view. I had a difficult time walking too far, so I would take breaks on a few benches along the way. The week went by fast and on Friday, we had to drive Joe back to the airport. I was happy to be going home because I still was feeling quite fatigued, my stomach was hurting on and off, and the weather was chilly. It was a nice trip, but it was difficult for me to recover on the road. When we got to Michigan, we stopped to see Thomas. I was so excited to see Thomas. I was extremely worried about him when we were on our trip because he had a bad cold. I was thankful to be home. Spending this time with my family meant the world to me. I was determined to go on this vacation because my family will always have the memories for a lifetime.

Home Sweet Home

I was still recovering from the virus. I had a visit with my family doctor on Thursday to evaluate my recovery from COVID. He was pleased by how well I was doing and suggested I start moving more to strengthen my lung capacity. He drew some laboratory blood work that all came back nearly normal. I decided to hit the gym to see what shape I was in. I tried the bike and was pleased that I was able to do a one-hour workout. I was also having back pain and left lower quadrant pain, so I went to my chiropractor, Dr. Brady, who always gets me back to normal. I also scheduled a PET scan before I started back on chemotherapy as suggested by the doctor at U of M hospital. The results made me quite upset. There was a new lymph node tumor that appeared and there was obstruction of the left kidney with a dilated left renal collecting system, suggesting renal failure. We had been watching this kidney for quite some time, but it really hit me when the radiologist suggested renal failure. Dave and I needed answers to many questions. We were set up with a virtual visit with an associate of Dr. Krauss since he was not available. We were told that I needed to get back on treatment as soon as possible and obtain a consultation with a urologist for a stent placement into the ureter to open the blockage. Dave was a blessing from God, called a colleague he trusted for further information. He also discussed the PET scan with my oncologist here in town. He immediately set me up to have an ultrasound of the area that was blocked. The ultrasound confirmed that the left kidney was not draining properly. In the meantime, I called my family doctor to give me some reassurance to have a stent placement, and he confirmed that would be my best option. Dave called back the urologist to discuss the results and I was scheduled for a stent the next day. I was in a panic state at this point thinking about all the possible complications. I was not in a good place after everything I had been through within the last month and six years of having cancer. I prayed to God and asked Him to calm me down. God has always guided me and given me the strength to get through life challenges. God did say, "In this world you will have trouble. But take heart! I have overcome the world." There is evil here on this earth, sin does exist, but we are not to live life for what we obtain here on earth but to focus on spending eternity with God in Heaven. "Do not store up for yourselves treasures on earth, where moths and vermin destroy, and where thieves break in and steal. But store up for yourselves treasures in heaven, where moths and vermin do not destroy, and where thieves do not break in and steal. For where your treasure is, there your heart will be also." I believe God has a plan for me. My surgery was set for 1p.m. Friday and Joe arrived at 8:30 a.m. I saw him pull up and my heart was filled with joy. The smile on his face told me everything and I gave him a great big hug and kiss when he came through the door. I was so thankful he made it home safe before we had to leave for the surgical center. Due to COVID restrictions, only David could come in with me. I couldn't eat or drink after midnight, but I made Dave and Joe waffles and coffee. I gave Joshua a great big hug and kiss before he left for school. We had a wonderful morning talking and spending time before we left for the surgical center in Port Huron. I gave Joe another huge hug and kiss, we all prayed together, and he reassured me everything was going to be fine. When we arrived, the lady at the desk checked me in, I completed the necessary paperwork, so as soon a nurse came to take me back, I gave Dave a big hug and kiss, and walked back with the nurse. She had me sign all the consents for the surgery, had me change into a hospital gown, and put a surgical cap over my hair. Then while she was getting me prepared for surgery the anesthesiologist, Dr. Hussain and the surgeon, Dr. Coury came back to evaluate me. I knew Dr. Hussain from working at River District Hospital. He was so kind and gentle during his evaluation. He told me my right lower lung field still had rhonchi due to the inflammation from the COVID infection. He asked my medical history and was amazed what I had to endure over the last six years. He noticed I was visibly shaken from telling him this story, so he was kind enough to ask me if I needed something to relax me before I went into surgery. I was given 2mg of Versed to help relax me, but when I turned to look at the monitor to see how high my blood pressure was, it was a good call on his part. Dr. Coury then came to explain the surgical procedure with a visual explanation of how the blockage causes the fluid to back up using the IV tubing. I am a visual person and that put me at ease. I had full confidence that he would be able to get the stent through the blockage. The nurses were compassionate and even allowed Dave to come back to sit with me. Dr. Hussain and Dave were having a great discussion about the medical profession. Again, he asked me if the medicine he gave me helped, and I told him I still felt a bit anxious. I had been through so many obstacles during such a short period of time, I didn't want to be wheeled into the operating room in a panic state. He gave me another 2mg of Versed and they wheeled me back. When I got there, they had me move to the surgical cart, strapped my arms down, and Dr. Hussain put me to sleep. I woke up back in the recovery area and was greeted by my nurse who gave me a cup of coffee and a graham crackers. She told me to get dressed when I was ready, and she would walk me out to the car where Dave was waiting. The nurses all got a good laugh when they saw I stripped my bed of the linen. I told them that I was a nurse and missed working so this was therapeutic for me. I gave the nurse a hug before I got into the car, and we made our way back home. Dave told me that Dr. Coury talked to him after my surgery and was pleased with the outcome. The only issue I had to deal with post-op was the pressure, frequency, and pain during urination. This was a normal experience after a surgery like this. Joshua was home from school when we arrived and was happy to see me and know everything went well. The best part of my day was when Joseph and Thomas came home from golfing. They had a good time together and this made me feel so Blessed. We eventually got a pizza for dinner, prayed before our meal, talked, and laughed. Later that evening we got Dairy Queen and watched television. Thomas and Joshua spent time talking and laughing before Thomas had to drive back to his apartment. The sad part for me was that I didn't know when we would be able to see Joe again since he was getting a job in Massachusetts. We watched a movie on tv and ended up going to bed for the night. I was praising God for all He did for me and for reminding me of His love.

Time to Rest

I tried to accept that chemotherapy would be a significant part of my life and I must give this to God. Dr. Kahn gave me an extra week to recover from surgery. I was in a lot of pain, had to pee often, and started to feel down after the boys left. I spent most of the time on the couch resting and trying to get better. I was upset because my treatment fell on Joshua's birthday, Tuesday, May 4. We decided to celebrate it on Sunday as a family. He wanted all his friends to come over on Friday and one of them spend the night. I was upset with Dave because he was planning on going to Lansing for a baseball tournament that same evening. He wanted me to come with him, but I didn't want to leave Joshua alone with all his friends coming over. I was in no shape to go with him to the tournament. I thought he would stay home but one of the coaches couldn't be there so Dave felt obligated to help. This did not make me happy at all, so I spent a lot of time praying. I didn't want to waste my time being angry. I didn't want to be upset with Dave because I knew his heart is good. He doesn't do anything to hurt me, and

I know he loves me with all his heart. I just felt sad because I didn't want us to be away from each other while I was recovering from my surgery. I was full of fear and anxiety leaving Joshua alone if I went with Dave. I felt overwhelmed with grief and then suddenly God came to me. I heard His gentle voice as I always do. He told me to go with my husband to the tournament. I didn't argue with God this time and suddenly the pain and all my issues seemed to get better by the end of the week. I surprised him and told him I was going with him. We both felt Joshua would be fine to be alone for one day with his friends. Dave and I went back to see the surgeon early Friday morning. He gave me medication for the urgency and frequency of urination. Dave was pleased I decided to go with him and so was I. The drive up to Lansing gave us time to talk, laugh, and listen to music. The hotel wasn't the nicest hotel, but I was just happy to be able to relax, watch television while Dave went to the first game. After the game, Dave picked me up and we went out to dinner with the coaches to celebrate our first win. The next morning Dave and I went out to breakfast before the next two games. I decided to go with Dave but stayed in the car because it was so cold outside, and to be near the bathroom. I made phone calls and waited for Dave to come to the car. He told me we won this game too. I decided to sit with the team for the third game and had an amazing time. I talked and laughed with all the parents while watching the game. The game was exciting, and we pulled off the win and got a trophy. I had such a good time that I ended up driving the two-hour drive home so Dave could relax. Joshua was home resting on the couch when we arrived. He had a lot of fun with his friends. I was proud of him for being so responsible while we were gone. Thomas came home Sunday, so we took Joshua out to celebrate his birthday at the Lebanese Grill. We came home and had cake and ice cream. We gave him a set of beginner's golf clubs for his birthday which made him happy. The weekend turned out so much better than I thought. I realized that if God loves me so much then I can trust that everything will turn out fine. God will get me through the tough times and lead me to a better place. My faith was growing more and more, to have less doubts, and have confidence in my belief in a loving God. In all my experiences over the years dealing with cancer, I realized that cancer could take away my health, but it can't take away the love I have for my family.

Cancer Can't Take Away Time with Joe

I was excited to spend a weekend with Joe after his move to Massachusetts. Despite my ongoing chemotherapy treatments, my body aches, all the issues from years of cancer, and roller coaster of emotions, I realized that spending time with my family is vital. I was not going to allow cancer to take away time spent with my son. I was determined to show him that despite how I felt, I would show him how I overcame all the obstacles from cancer treatment. It was also our 26th wedding anniversary on May 27th. I felt it was more important to support Joe with his move to Massachusetts, and new job, so we spent the weekend to visit him. We had to get home Monday because my treatment was Tuesday, Joshua had to go back to school, and David had to go back to work. Fortunately, I was able to get my laboratory work done on Wednesday morning before we left so the results would be back in time for me to have my treatment. Thankfully, both Thomas and Joshua were able to drive a few hours which split up the driving among us all. I was extremely tired and slept in the car for much of the drive. The weather did not cooperate on this trip. We drove through rain, and the temperature dropped to the 50's which is chilly for May. I was hoping for warmer weather, but nothing was going to deter my excitement to visit my son. Upon our arrival, we checked in the hotel just in time for Joe to get off work. We stayed at a Springhill Suite which is another amazing hotel with great service, amenities, cleanliness, and comfort. The room had a desk for Dave to do his office work. He still must make calls, does medication refills, looks up laboratory results, and communicate with his staff about issues that arrive. We decided to go to dinner in downtown Andover, about 10 minutes from Joe's new apartment. I ordered chicken parmesan which came with three breasts of chicken covered with parmesan cheese over pasta noodles. The dinner was fantastic, warm, and I ended up eating only one chicken breast with a small portion of pasta. I took the rest of my meal back to Joe's apartment along with Dave's chicken piccata meal. We didn't stay long there because I was extremely tired from the long day's ride and wanted to get back to the hotel. We were quite upset to hear that the moving company delayed Joe's furniture until the next Saturday. I thought it would have been great to help him unload all the boxes and arrange his furniture. Instead, Dave and I put away a pile of laundry he decided to throw on the floor. I gave him a hard time about it while I was hanging up and folding his laundry. I figured, it's not about the laundry, it's about showing him that I'm still his mom, I still can help him despite my cancer, and it made me feel I'm needed. Even though I have cancer, I am always thinking of ways to honor God in my attitude, demeanor, character, as a wife, as a mom, and to all the people in my life I encounter. We decided to visit downtown Boston on Friday to tour the city while walking the brick paved road to Bunker Hill, a museum, and a commissioned ship at the harbor. Dave didn't want to risk driving and finding parking in such a large city, so we decided to take the train. I was happy to relax on the train and enjoyed the ride to the city. When we got off the train, we found the walking trail that went on for miles before we arrived at our planned destination. Along the way we walked up and down hills to observe historical sites like a graveyard that had people buried there from the 1800's. I was too tired to go with the boys but sat on the steps that led up to the site. We walked quite a way, it was getting cold, I had lower abdominal pressure that made me go to the bathroom frequently, and my feet, hips, and body were hurting all over. I sat on the stairs with my hoodie over my head, all bundled, and waited for the boys to finish. We continued our walk along miles of buildings that were unique and historical. Joshua loves history and was thrilled to be there. He was so excited he told me the entire story about the war and all the battles that led up to our independence in America. I never liked history, but Joshua sure makes it interesting as he tells so many stories. The weather was getting colder, windy, and started to sprinkle rain as we were walking over a bridge to get to a historical ship, the USS Constitution.

This ship was used in the war of 1812 and is still in commission. You had to go through security to enter the ship, but I was so cold and exhausted that I decided to warm up in the museum across the parking lot and hit the bathroom again. I figured they would take some time touring the ship and climbing down a steep ladder to tour the lower level which I was unable to do at the time. I didn't complain because I was thrilled to be with my family, so I enjoyed every minute despite my medical issues. The boys eventually found me, and we walked over to have dinner at a restaurant nearby. After dinner, we walked a few more blocks back to the train station, back to our car, and dropped Thomas and Joe back at the apartment. We were all tired, cold, and wanted to chill the rest of the evening after such a long day in the city. The next day the weather was awful, it was freezing cold, raining, and I was hurting all over from the long walk the day before. I decided to do some laundry and rest with Joshua while he was doing his homework. The boys went shopping for house supplies for Joe. I was so tired, I fell asleep for hours, but it felt good to get our laundry done while we were there. They came back with a card table, chairs, small pot, pan, and some cooking utensils. We decided to go out to pizza for dinner to a place ten minutes away. It was the best pizza I have ever had. After dinner, we stayed a while with Joe and Thomas before we went back to the hotel. The next morning, we went to IKEA for items Joe needed for his apartment. Joe bought a coffee table, television stand, a set of glasses, a towel bar for his bathroom, and a toilet brush. When we got back, I finished our last load of laundry while the boys put together the furniture Joe bought. After they finished putting together the furniture, we decided to go out to dinner. Joshua picked out a local place not too far away. We had the great dinner conversation about trusting the Lord when we're facing challenges. I was emotional when we went back to Joe's apartment because this was our last night. Thomas had to pack his things up to spend the night with us in the hotel, because we were leaving quite early in the morning. I finished the laundry then sat with Joseph in his room to say goodbye. The tears flowed down my face as I told him how special he was to me, and how much I loved him. I gave him a huge hug and kiss goodbye and gathered my things to go back to the hotel. The boys all said goodbye too which made me feel even sadder. I love my family and appreciate this time even more while I keep having more issues with my cancer journey. I don't know how much time I have left, so every moment I have with my family is precious. When we left his apartment, I cried all the way to the elevator, but just before I left, I gave Joe one last hug and kiss goodbye. This was extremely difficult for me to leave my son here so far away from home. As much as it hurts, I must be strong for him to be successful in his new job. He worked so hard, and it took him a long time to get to this point. I realized another door opened for him and it will lead to another one, so who knows exactly where he will end up. I'm incredibly proud of him.

I know Joseph has a good relationship with the Lord and no matter what happens to me, I know he will be successful, and God will guide him every step of the way. I did my best to raise him in a Christian home, but the world sometimes wants to disregard everything I taught him with the culture we live in. This is when I get down on my knees and pray to God to guide me through all my fears and worry. I can't help but worry with the evil in this world that wants to divide the family and conquer it. Joe's made good choices and has proven to me that he will be a leader. I can't ask more than this for my son, and even though I shed tears, I also have great joy in my heart. We left the following morning with me shedding more tears. I had a difficult time saying goodbye and telling him exactly how much he means to me, how much I love him, how much I want the world for him, and how much I want him to continue his walk with the Lord. Maybe he already knows all of this, but in my heart, I will always have a special place for him, I will always be his mother, and he will always be a Blessing. Thankfully after a 15-hour car ride, we made it home safely. I had to get up early in the morning to get ready for my chemotherapy treatment. I thanked God for this special time with my family but having Thomas and Joshua home with me was also a special Blessing. Cancer can take away my health but it CAN'T take away the time I spend with my son Joe.

Cancer Can't Take Away Joy with Thomas

In addition to Joe moving to Massachusetts, Thomas also moved into a one-bedroom apartment and started the process for applying to medical school. Thomas is my middle child, so he lives in the shadows of Joseph, and probably doesn't get all the attention of the last child, Joshua. I love all my boys equally. Thomas is a child sent from God who is driven, has a heart for the Lord, and I must admit it, we are a lot alike in our temperaments. What I love about all my boys is that we can have a heart-to-heart discussion about life, values, politics, school, but no matter how differently we may see things, they know without a doubt the love I have for them. Thomas wears his heart on his sleeve, and he pushes himself harder than I can ask him. He also played baseball for many years but decided to give it up when he went to college. He wanted to follow his dad's footsteps with a desire to enter medical school. This is no easy goal, especially with the amount of extra-curricular work, high grade-point average, and MCAT score that is required for entrance. Thomas did everything possible to get accepted into medical school. He decided to obtain a degree as a Biomedical Engineer as a prerequisite, which is one of the most difficult programs to complete. He amazed me and did very well throughout the years with keeping a high grade-point average, volunteering at Karmanos Hospital, and made good choices along the way. I was especially proud of him because of his determination, and he had to put in a significant amount of effort to obtain this accomplishment. There were times I got on my knees and prayed for him to stay safe, healthy, and do well in school. Many kids enter college and think it's time to party, so eventually their grades start slipping, and they end up failing some of their classes, changing majors, or dropping out of school. Thomas had some fun living in Detroit near the downtown area with all his new friends he met, but it didn't alter his focus on academic excellence. He even had to attend classes in the summer to keep up with the program while he volunteered. By volunteering at Karmanos Hospital, he was able to relate to the cancer patients with being a part of my journey. He became empathetic as he listened to their stories on their way to the cancer center. He enjoyed this experience because it prepared him for what challenges he would face in medical school. He also shadowed an Orthopedic Surgeon, a Family Practice Physician, and my cousin, Mike Balok, an Ophthalmologist. This gave him more experience with what doctor's face when seeing patients in a busy practice. Though he was doing fabulous, I was always worried about his stress level with taking on too much, especially during the COVID-19 pandemic. The school campus was closed for over a semester, so he had to adjust to doing his classes on-line in his apartment with little to no socialization. He had to push forward, continue school despite the world going off the deep end, and find a way to get through this crisis. I missed him terribly just as I did Joseph when he was away. I spent many nights crying myself to sleep as I prayed to God. God did comfort me through this crisis, and soon things started to open, doctors were finding protocols that worked, hospital admissions started to decline, and life slowly got back to normal. Thomas remained taking classes on-line during this time and looked forward to his senior year back on campus. He finished his junior year with success, saddened by saying goodbye to his roommate who moved out. Thomas was forced to find a one-bedroom apartment because he couldn't find another student who was willing to share a two-bedroom apartment. Dave and I assisted him with packing up, cleaning, and moving all his belongings to his new apartment and to our house. Thomas was not going to attend college this summer, so he was finally able to come home. I couldn't be happier even though he decided to travel to Florida the following week with a group of his friends. I didn't want him to leave again, but I felt that he deserved to get away for a week with how much he poured himself into his studies over the last three years. He finally was going to be home, and it made me excited to spend this time with him. I didn't even mind doing his laundry and cooking more food, because I felt so much joy. The best part of him coming home was we were going to visit Joseph, and we planned a vacation in North Carolina on the beach in July. When he was home, he spent numerous hours on the application process for medical school. He had to write an essay, fill out forms, submit letters of recommendations, transcripts, and complete all the requirements for medical school applications. We prayed for him countless times and had many discussions about allowing God to shine His light on this situation. I couldn't have been prouder of him at this moment for all the effort he put into this process. I felt that if God wants him to become a doctor, nothing will prevent it from happening. Dave and I spent so much time encouraging him to be strong, give this to the Lord, and continue his life as normal. I know God has a plan for all of us, and He would guide Thomas through this. I know that I serve an awesome God despite the obstacles we face daily. In our trials, God shows up and guides us through our problems, so we must trust that He will not abandon us. God is a good God. Every day I wake up and thank Him, for His Grace is sufficient for us. I will honor Him in all I do and give Him all the glory. Thomas will succeed in this life because he is a bright, talented, passionate young man who loves the Lord. I know the Lord will be there with him during this challenge and all the challenges he will face throughout his life. Cancer can take away my health but it CAN"T take away my joy with Thomas.

Cancer Can't Stop Me from Smiling and Laughing with Joshua

When Joshua was born, I held him tight in my arms praying to God to always be with him. I was exhausted with two boys and wanted to feel the joy of this child being the last one we were going to have. I bonded with him, prayed over him, and felt a special sense of peace as I looked in his beautiful eyes. I had this feeling overwhelm me that he was going to be an incredibly special child of God and was going to do great things. I love all my boys, but Joshua was my last baby, and I was thankful he was healthy. He didn't fall into the footsteps of the boys with sports, but that was fine with Dave and I. Joshua loved music and was extremely gifted playing his instruments. He also was gifted with a great memory and was a sponge to learn about freighters, presidents, history, and geography. He astonished the teachers when he helped at the concession stand to know exactly how much to charge and how much change to give back. He was friendly, energetic, and always willing to help where needed. He would also help Joseph in our church with the audio-visual set up for our church service. I was so proud of both serving in this role. When he was older, he assisted with ushering, but the best was when he played in the band. Joshua played the trumpet, bassoon, and later taught himself to play the bass for Sunday services. I just beamed with joy when he would play with the band, they were all extremely talented. He also got a job on the spot at a golf course when he was only 16 years old. Working at the golf course was a dirty job because he had to bring in the carts, clean them, and then fill them with gasoline for the next day. He enjoyed the job and made a decent salary for the summer months. Joshua's best friend was Trevor who became like a son to me. He was here often with their group of friends, and I enjoyed every moment watching them play games, cards, swimming in the canal, and just hanging out as a group of kids. We took Trevor with us to Florida this past March, and I learned just how much he could eat. Trevor and Joshua had most of their classes together in high-school and are probably the smartest kids in the school, or at least the funniest. They had a riot in chemistry with their teacher. He had a lot of fun with them during all the experiments. Joshua is an all-around kid who loves the Lord, is a great person to others, is strong-willed, but a gentle heart. He always puts a smile on my face and makes me laugh. When I was diagnosed, he would write to me cards that brought me to tears. One card came from the entire class with a get-well message. Joshua always knew how to touch my heart, especially when I was feeling down. We would have adult conversations. He would tell me about God's love, and it always made me feel so much better. I cherish those talks because it was as if God Himself was talking to me through this young boy. He made me feel that everything was going to be okay. Cancer can take away my health but it CAN"T take away the smiles and laughter Joshua gives to me.

I'm so proud of all my boys for sharing their faith with me during my illness. I know without a doubt just how much they all love me. All my boys cheer me up when I am down and support me during the difficult moments with their love. I don't know how I would do it without my three boys. They are all unique individuals but their love for God, family, and each other is what keeps me fighting. I fight for them because I want to share in on all their special moments. I'm thankful to God for every moment I've had with them. This year I witnessed so much of their accomplishments. Joe obtaining a chemical engineering job, Thomas applying to medical school, and Joshua being selected for drum major, student council president, scoring the highest SAT in his high school, and getting accepted to the University of Michigan School of Engineering. These are milestone accomplishments that I will always cherish and look forward to so many more. I pray that God gives me the courage and strength to continue this battle with colon cancer. I pray that God gives me many more years to spend with my boys so I can see their future dreams come true. I know without a doubt that they will be successful and continue their relationship with the Lord. I also know that even during the most difficult times they may face, they will turn to God for guidance and comfort. Having God, a part of our family brings me great joy, peace of mind, and comfort. I am Blessed with my three boys, and I ask God to continue to Bless them, wrap His loving arms around them, and shine His light upon them so that they will continue to walk in His presence. Life is short, we must learn to love God and love others in all we do. My boys are the greatest gift from God who have filled my life with love.

Cancer Can't Stop Love and 26 Years of Marriage

We celebrated our 26th anniversary May 27, 2021, on our way to visit Joe in Andover, Massachusetts. I believe God was instrumental in bringing Dave and I together from the moment my head nurse said, "I have this guy I would like you to meet". My only thought was, "sure", and didn't think much of it after two failed relationships. My head nurse continued to tell me more about Dave and it sparked an interest. She told me he was a Family Practice Physician, Lebanese, and a great person. She set us up on a blind date through a friend of hers who also was trying to match make him with a nice girl. We all met at a restaurant, and it was love at first sight. He was handsome, kind, funny, dressed well, and we had a lot in common. He drove me home that night and I wrote my number on his business card which he still has saved until today. His car was spotless, he was so polite and friendly, and he called me back when he said he would. Before I met Dave, I would wheel my mom to the chapel at St. John Hospital. I prayed I would find a man with a heart for the Lord, and he would bring me closer to God. Dave was the man God sent me. It didn't take too much time to figure it out after dating him for less than a year. We had so much in common with our Christian values, financial spending habits, love for family, and our Lebanese culture was a plus. We both loved the Lebanese food, and his mom could cook up a feast. Dave's family welcomed me with open arms. Dave and I spent a lot of time together as he was fixing up the house. The joke was if I would help him dig a ditch to put a drainpipe in, he would buy me a ring. Well, that evening when he came home the ditch was done, and he bought me a ring. Dave and I loved each other and grew more in love with each other over the years. Love is more than intimacy, materialism, but giving oneself to the other. There are times we struggled with different views, but we always would temper our differences with God's help. We learned about Grace during our arguments. We always put our family first. We may have had our careers, hobbies, interests, but we always spent time worshiping on Sunday as a family, doing family things, and being thankful for everything. Throughout all the years we were married, cancer has taught us how to love each other more. I would not be able to get through this journey if I didn't have David as my husband. God has Blessed me with an amazing man. Cancer can take away my health but it CAN"T take away the love between Dave and I.

Loving God: Living with Cancer

Yes, I was diagnosed with cancer, and this was a game changer for how I looked at life. I have faced many challenges in my life: sadness, depression, anxiety, but cancer was different. Cancer brought me to my knees. God had a whole new meaning to me now. Sadly, I look back and regret not knowing and loving God like I do now. I realized that my life was now limited to a timeframe that smacked me straight in my face, not knowing how many days, months, years I would be here on earth. When I put this into perspective, I needed my Savior. I prayed for God to move Heaven and Earth to keep me alive so I could be here with my family. I got down on my knees and cried out to God so hard, my stomach hurt. I asked God to forgive me for all my sins and promised to devote my life to Him. I promised Him that if I lived through this cancer that I would live to turn people toward Him. I pray nobody ever gets to this point of desperation, but I felt I didn't have time to waste. I was losing everything I worked my whole life for around me. I had to quit both my jobs as a Registered Nurse in the ICU and as a Clinical Instructor. I spent over 30 years working in the hospital and I had to give it all up for cancer. This hurt me terribly and I felt so much grief. I was active in the school and in my church, so I had to limit being available to volunteering in my community. My new life was filled with doctor visits, exams, scans, tests, chemotherapy, radiation therapy, surgeries, nausea, weakness, and depression. Many people would have thrown in the towel, become angry, bitter, and given up, but I knew that God would guide me through this. My relationship with God was always good, but like I said, He was not always front and center. I put God front and center now. I wanted to be in control. You just can't do that when you have cancer. You must realize that every breath you take is because God allowed you to take it. You must realize that nothing here on earth is without God's hand in it, except sin. God only does good, everything in my life that was good was the result of God's Blessings. When you have cancer, you need God more than ever, and I knew I needed Him to get me through this crisis. I was facing life and death decisions; I didn't know how long I'd be here. Nothing was certain, except I had to fight back all the negative emotions, turn to God for my courage and strength, and push forward. My family meant the world to me, so I had to be strong for them. I didn't want them to take the brunt to what I was going through, so I needed God now more than ever. People would always say how strong I was, how much faith I

Loving God: Living with Cancer

Yes, I was diagnosed with cancer, and this was a game changer for how I looked at life. I have faced many challenges in my life: sadness, depression, anxiety, but cancer was different. Cancer brought me to my knees. God had a whole new meaning to me now. Sadly, I look back and regret not knowing and loving God like I do now. I realized that my life was now limited to a timeframe that smacked me straight in my face, not knowing how many days, months, years I would be here on earth. When I put this into perspective, I needed my Savior. I prayed for God to move Heaven and Earth to keep me alive so I could be here with my family. I got down on my knees and cried out to God so hard, my stomach hurt. I asked God to forgive me for all my sins and promised to devote my life to Him. I promised Him that if I lived through this cancer that I would live to turn people toward Him. I pray nobody ever gets to this point of desperation, but I felt I didn't have time to waste. I was losing everything I worked my whole life for around me. I had to quit both my

Loving God: Living with Cancer

jobs as a Registered Nurse in the ICU and as a Clinical Instructor. I spent over 30 years working in the hospital and I had to give it all up for cancer. This hurt me terribly and I felt so much grief. I was active in the school and in my church, so I had to limit being available to volunteering in my community. My new life was filled with doctor visits, exams, scans, tests, chemotherapy, radiation therapy, surgeries, nausea, weakness, and depression. Many people would have thrown in the towel, become angry, bitter, and given up, but I knew that God would guide me through this. My relationship with God was always good, but like I said, He was not always front and center. I put God front and center now. I wanted to be in control. You just can't do that when you have cancer. You must realize that every breath you take is because God allowed you to take it. You must realize that nothing here on earth is without God's hand in it, except sin. God only does good, everything in my life that was good was the result of God's Blessings. When you have cancer, you need God more than ever, and I knew I needed Him to get me through this crisis. I was facing life and death decisions; I didn't know how long I'd be here. Nothing was certain, except I had to fight back all the negative emotions, turn to God for my courage and strength, and push forward. My family meant the world to me, so I had to be strong for them. I didn't want them to take the brunt to what I was going through, so I needed God now more than ever. People would always say how strong I was, how much faith I

Loving God: Living with Cancer

had, and say what an inspiration I was to them. Well, the truth is, I'm not that strong. It was God who lifted me up every day through every blood test, scan, test, surgery, chemotherapy and radiation treatment, doctor visit, and the roller coaster of emotions. It was God who I relied on to guide me and the doctors to make the right decisions. It was God who comforted me at night when I would cry my eyes out in deep hurt, confusion, and pain. I give God all the glory. I relied on God to calm me down, give me courage, and love me as His child. I honestly don't know how anyone can get through a serious illness without God.

God didn't purposefully give me cancer, but even if it was a part of His plan, I have two choices: ask God for help or do it on my own. I chose to turn to God to hold me up and give me the tools I needed to get through this crisis. God sends good people your way to help you so you're not alone. I can't even tell you how many good people are praying for me and my family. They send me cards, texts, phone calls, gifts, and so much love that I feel the presence of God surround me. The doctors are gifted in their knowledge to know what treatment options would work for my individual needs. I know God sent me good doctors, nurses, technicians, and all the people who work in the hospital setting. I may experience nausea and vomiting, but God is a part of the making of medicines that will curb those side effects. God gave me the Blessing of going to the University of Michigan hospital for a team of highly qualified physicians who oversee my case. Most importantly, God gave me a family, especially my husband Dave, to love me even when I'm not so lovable. God works miracles through people to make this journey worth it and He asks nothing in return. Jesus died on the cross for me, and I humbly accept His Grace. For His Grace is sufficient for me and all that I need. His Grace is what empowers me to hold my head up high, feel worthy to live, and want to give back to this world. I have a whole new meaning to living now than I ever had before. There is nothing I could desire more than His love and to spend eternity with Him. I could live for one more day or ten more years and without Christ, I am nothing. It's taken me over 50 years of my life to learn some of these lessons and I'm praying for you to learn them sooner. God loves you; He wants you to love Him. Being a mother and wife, I understand this love with my family. I would do anything for them to make their life better. I would move heaven and earth to keep them safe, secure, and feel loved. God does the same for us too. He gave up His life for our sins, even when we reject Him, He doesn't reject us. He's waiting for us to acknowledge that we can't do it alone, we need Him. We need to get to know Him, trust Him, and turn our lives over to Him. We may need to make some changes from the old ways to filter out our sinful nature, but this will lead you down a better path to salvation. Cancer can destroy your body, but it doesn't have to destroy who you are in Jesus Christ. Cancer can leave you in pain, suffering, and sorrow, but Jesus leaves you with passion, purpose, and peace. You can live with cancer, but you cannot live without God. I have cancer but I have a God who takes the "cer" out of cancer and says, I can! I can beat this! I can be the best person I can be. I can me a wife, mom, friend, and nurse. I can be anything I want to be during this disease, but I can be God's child and lean on His understanding and not mine. Cancer will not destroy me, define me, nor will it defeat me! I serve an amazing God who will love me through all of this. I know God will take care of all my needs, especially my family. Nothing is impossible with God, He has a plan, and I will submit myself to Jesus Christ. I can live with cancer because I love God. I love God with all my heart, all my mind, and all my soul, and I love others as God loves me. Living with cancer and loving God is possible. All you must do is be willing to ask God to come into your life. God loves you and is waiting for you to follow Him. God Bless you, may God wrap His loving arms around you, may He shine His loving face upon you, and may your life be filled with His Glory forever more. Amen!